Breaking Through

Getting Past the Stuck Points in Your Life

edited by

Barbara Stanny

with Oriana Green

POWERFUL WOMAN PRESS

Published in the United States of America by
Powerful Woman Press
2023 E. Sims Way, Suite 328
Port Townsend, WA 98368
www.BreakingThroughBook.com

First edition, September 2006
Printed in the U.S.A.
ISBN: 1-934126-01-2
ISBN-13: 978-1-93412-601-1

Table of Contents

Preface

I always hated those times I felt stuck. And they happened a lot. I'd be sailing through life when suddenly, inexplicably, I'd get stopped in my tracks, as if I'd run smack dab into an invisible wall. I'd lose my bearings along with my bravado, my focus as well as my footing, and never be quite sure exactly what happened, nor if it would ever end. Those stuck points varied in intensity and duration. Sometimes I was back on my feet in only a few days. Other times I was down for the count, convinced my life had come to a screeching halt, my career was finished, all chance at happiness gone forever. No matter how long they lasted, these were always very dark, dreaded periods.

But that was before I had my epiphany, before I came to understand that every stuck point has a valuable purpose.

The epiphany

I was in the gym, working out with a trainer, about to do a chest press with no added weight. I lay flat on my back and grabbed the bar, pushed it high above my body, then lowered it to just above my chest and back up, repeating the exercise 12 times. No problem. It was easy. Then my trainer put five pound weights on each end of the bar. I felt the difference immediately. By the second repetition, my arms were quivering. The third time I lowered the bar to my chest, those extra pounds felt more like tons. The bar wouldn't budge. I strained. I struggled. I was clearly stuck. My ego felt deflated. My trainer saw it differently.

"That's how you build muscles," he explained, "by getting past the stuck point."

Sure enough, in the next couple of weeks, with the resolve of a warrior in battle, I eventually could do 12 consecutive reps with the heavier weight without flinching. But my trainer didn't let me rest in my glory. Instead, he added more weight. And sure enough, I was instantly at a new stuck point.

But instead of dismay, I felt determined. I realized that getting past this new stuck point was an opportunity for me to build my muscles, boost my endurance and push myself to a new level of strength.

At that moment, the weights became an obvious metaphor for life. Getting past my previous stuck points was precisely how I have grown physically, mentally and emotionally stronger. It is how I have built my confidence muscles, experienced higher levels of achievement and discovered new possibilities I could never have predicted. What I once dreaded as a dismal period, I could now welcome as a vital stage in the process of growth.

A love/hate relationship

Still, understanding, even appreciating a stuck point is one thing. Accepting one is another. And navigating one gracefully is something else all together. After all, the goal of the stuck point is to get past it. Despite my realization that every stuck point has an important function, whenever I'm in one, I'm prone to forget what it is. Instead of seeing immobility as a temporary but fertile period preceding a growth spurt, I often find myself trying to rush through it or berating myself for my inertia.

Even though I understand it's value, the challenge continues to be learning to acknowledge, honor and harness the power of the stuck point, skillfully riding it like a wave to a distant shore.

The result

My colleague and co-editor, Oriana Green, and I were brainstorming one day about creating an anthology, and that's when the idea for this book was born. I thought of all the amazing women I knew who have not only successfully navigated their own stuck points, but are in the business of helping others do so as well. I wanted to know how these women did it, what advice they might have for me, so that others, like yourself, could benefit. It's the same reason I've written all my books—to learn from those who have prevailed.

We wanted to offer a toolbox of ideas, tips, exercises, meditations and processes to help you get unstuck and back on your road to your success.

As I read the contributions that poured in, I often got chills. Each submission was unique and valuable in its own right. A few made me laugh out loud, while others brought tears to my eyes. The essays filled me with optimism, insight and encouragement, and they represent a treasure trove of wisdom that only comes from hard won experience. But what touched me most was how surprisingly candid many women were, how willingly they revealed their own vulnerabilities.

More than 60 women responded and reassured me that I'm not the only who gets stuck on a regular basis. And they reminded me that when put in perspective, every stuck point is actually a prelude to new starting point. I was inspired, captivated and buoyed by hope that the next time I find myself in what feels like a dark, stagnant hole, I'll curl up with this book and remember what my personal trainer taught me years ago. Getting past the stuck point is how we build our muscles.

I have the utmost gratitude and appreciation for the women who have contributed to this book. They have provided all of us with some very powerful tools—but it's up to each of us to put them to use. If we can embrace the uncertainty, endure the discomfort and use these tools to push past our barriers, we will discover there's tremendous power in every stuck point. And it's the power we can use to create the life of our dreams.

~Barbara Stanny, co-editor

Introduction

I've been seriously, down-a-dark-hole stuck more times than I care to remember, which is why this project excites me so much—I can see the potential to help many people in a whole range of situations. We can all use new perspectives on our challenges. Whether you find yourself stuck in an unfulfilling career, in a relationship that's gone south or floundering in a project that threatens to drown you in details, you're sure to find useful advice in this book.

You'll discover wisdom from more than 60 insightful professional women, who share hundreds of tips, tricks and tools for getting unstuck. You'll hear from personal coaches, therapists, financial advisors and authors, as well as from practitioners of more exotic systems of thought, so I encourage you to keep an open mind as you consider these offerings.

There are articles about finding support, examining family patterns, coping with loss and grief, exploring various meditative practices and unlocking your creativity. You'll receive tips about spending your money more wisely, ending self-sabotage and handling your precious time better. *Breaking Through* also contains exercises for evaluating your goals, dealing with your excuses and tuning into the power of gratitude. You'll even find some suggestions that will get you up and moving and examining your world in a new way.

Each essay is short enough to be enjoyed during those chunks of time that might be otherwise wasted—in waiting rooms, in the car outside your kids' school—or for you multi-taskers, listened to while working out or whipping up dinner.

In fact, I even suggest having some fun with this advice. One way would be to use this book like an oracle—just open it up each day to a random page or audio track, and that's the tool you are supposed to explore on that day. You could even set an intention by saying: What do I need to know today to get past this stuck point? Then allow your intuition to guide you to the right message for that moment.

Or if you prefer a more systematic approach, you could read one piece every morning to inspire you to confront your challenges. That might be especially useful if you're in the midst of an ongoing stuck period.

All of these essays are catalysts for self-understanding and action. Pay special attention to any that may spark a negative reaction or resistance. These could be the ideas that offer the greatest opportunities for growth. Recognizing resistance is a good thing, as it shows at least part of you desires to change, and you're fighting the inner urge to remain in your comfort zone. Pushing through that resistance and entering your *dis*comfort zone is the direct path to your goals.

Finally, if after working through all these stimulating ideas for change you still find yourself stuck, then perhaps you need to examine what the payoffs are for you in clinging to that mindset. What are you gaining by stagnation? On some level, the known benefits of *not* moving ahead must outweigh the unknown benefits of change. Once you identify the payoffs, you can make a conscious decision about whether or not they are, indeed, worth delaying your growth.

These ideas are timeless. Think of this as a lifelong reference book, to be consulted whenever you feel yourself getting stuck. But most of all, I want to encourage you to really *use* this book—you can't get unstuck if you just add this book to your stack to be read *someday*. Start taking action *this* day!

~Oriana Green, co-editor

Note about the contributors

Inside this book you'll find wisdom from over 60 talented, professional women. To learn more about each of them, please refer to the contributors section beginning on Page 225. Also, you can learn even more about them at **www.BreakingThroughBook.com** which includes contact information, links to their email and website addresses.

The Gift of Being Stuck

By Harriett Simon Salinger

Everyone gets stuck . . .eventually. It's part of being human. But being stuck—not knowing which way to turn, what path to follow, what choices to make—is not always a cause for fear. Sometimes being stuck is an enormous gift, a blank slate, a welcome respite, a great opportunity.

Feeling stuck forces you to revisit your personal world and honor the sacred gift of life. You are compelled to examine and explore your present situation, to discover who you are, where you are, what forces are at play in your life, and what needs to change. If you never, ever feel stuck, then I wonder what kind of a life you're living.

While I'm not one of those "10 steps to solve anything" coaches—it's just not my style—let me suggest a few things to consider when you feel unable to move or make new and fresh choices.

❂ Be here now. Summon the courage to be present in the time and place in which you find yourself today. There's no other place to be . . . there's no other place you can be. Surrender to this very moment, this feeling, this reality. This is your starting point.

❂ Recognize that life does not proceed in a straight line. As the oceans have tides, so do our lives—there are starts and stops, ups and downs, peaks and valleys. But because we so desperately fear being stuck, we often rush ahead of where we can be, making the mistake of trying to push our "waves" before they are ready to be pushed. As with a becalmed sailboat, sometimes you simply have to wait until the energy is there to move with the waves.

❂ Be willing to lose your way. My favorite quotation is from the poet Galway Kinnell, who once said, "The first step shall be to lose the way." Are you willing to lose your way, to step into the unknown, to not know? Sometimes we simply "know" too much. We over-think and over-analyze, giving rise to fears and worry, which effectively locks us in jail cells of our own self-limitations. Recognizing the power of not knowing, of losing the way, is sometimes the greatest gift of being stuck—the key that can unlock our cell.

When I was in social work school at Columbia, I read *Common Human Needs* by Charlotte Towle, a mother of the social work profession. It's a classic tome written in 1925, but her words "always start where the client is" still resonate after all these years. I remembered her words during my time as a social worker; I remembered them as a psychotherapist; and I've remembered them as a personal coach for the past 11 years.

I invite you to start "where you are" by honoring your gift of being stuck as an important part of your journey in consciousness—an opportunity for you to embrace, rather than a cause for fear and worry.

Search for the Source

By Lois P. Frankel, Ph.D.

To get unstuck, you have to understand how you got stuck in the first place. My experience coaching hundreds of people around the world, is that most people get stuck when they over rely on skills and behaviors learned early in childhood. As children, we resiliently respond to implicit or explicit parental demands or requests by developing coping mechanisms. If the statistic is true that nine out of ten people come from some kind of dysfunctional family, then most of us employ behaviors that might have actually outlived their usefulness as we've progressed in our lives or careers. Here are some examples.

❂ Dad was a real task master. You learned early on that success was contingent upon working hard and keeping your nose to the grindstone. It's been a winning strategy up until now, but your current job requires different skills, like thinking more strategically or taking time to build strong, 360 degree relationships. You feel stuck because you fear working "less hard" will result in disaster.

❂ Mom always taught you that little girls were to be seen and not heard. As a result, teachers and bosses during your lifetime loved having you around—you presented no difficulties for them. But you've reached a point in your career where you notice promotions, plum assignments and perks are going to people who risk having their voices heard. You feel stuck because you fear you'll be seen as pushy and unladylike if you voice your opinions.

✪ As the oldest of five children in an alcoholic home, you learned to pay close attention to detail so you could take good care of your younger siblings. Partly as a result of this strength developed in childhood, you chose a career in accounting. All was going well until you were promoted to manager, and now people see you as picky and a micro-manager. You feel stuck because you don't know any other way to lead people.

Getting unstuck requires 1) giving yourself permission to move from childhood to adulthood; 2) realistically assessing those strengths you developed in childhood and identifying what new skills you need to learn to create greater balance in your repertoire; and 3) giving up the superstitious belief that if you do anything different something catastrophic will happen.

Here are some tips to help you get unstuck:

1. Enlist support. Ask a friend at work to help you develop a strategic plan for your department or help you to prepare a monthly budget.

2. Don't give up what you're good at—add new skills to the mix. This will contribute to a natural balance.

3. Take baby steps. If it's speaking up more that you're working on, don't start dominating meetings. Set a goal to give your opinion once or twice in every meeting.

4. Reassure the child within. We all have an inner child who sometimes over relies on old rules (i.e. always give 150%; always be polite; always think for yourself). It makes us fearful of doing something different. Assure her that you're in charge now, and you will make sure everything is well taken care of.

5. Be patient. It doesn't matter if it takes you a week, a month, or a year to get unstuck. Take the pressure off by allowing yourself to enjoy and learn from the journey.

Are You A Rebel?

By Pegine Echevarria

Are you a rebel? Do you fight against the rules? Do you want to do things your way? Do you discount others' advice? Maybe you know someone who is a rebel?

Movies have glamorized the bad boy image, the rebel. For those of you who have embraced the rebel attitude, you may need to acknowledge that your thoughts and behaviors have not resulted in the kind of life you wanted. The problem with being a rebel is that too often rebels are fighting the rules just because. There is no real plan for what you want to achieve. You just do not want to follow the rules.

I've met so many talented, skilled, phenomenal people who have rebelled against rules, protocol, processes and the natural laws of success, wealth and love. The result of all this was stress, anger, resentment, loneliness, and lack (of abundance, appreciation and opportunities).

Enough, I say. It's time for all you rebels to get over yourselves. (Okay, <u>our</u>selves. I was, and at times, still am, a rebel.) You need to take charge of your careers, your businesses, your teams and your lives by letting the rebel factor go. In fact, after years of introspection and having a few "aha"s along the way, I've come to realize the word REBEL really stands for:

R - Resisting
E - Excellence
B - By Not
E - Engaging
L - Leverage

R= RESIST

When you rebel you resist following the rules. There are umpteen reasons why you don't want to follow the rules. Perhaps you believe someone is out to get you, or you feel you know better, or that's true for you but not me! It could also be feeling you're not good enough. When you rebel, you resist what you perceive as conforming, giving in or succumbing. Everyone has been a rebel at one time or another. However, what you're really resisting is excellence.

E= EXCELLENCE

Excellence is achieved when you take action and perform as well as you possibly can. When there is resistance to following the steps, protocol or natural laws, it is impossible to achieve excellence. Yes, I know—some rules are limiting and stifling. You can take action and change them by following the rules of change, but by resisting the rules you are setting yourself up to encounter stress, anger, resentment, loneliness and lack. You lose power to change the rule or improve the process of implementation because you create resistance.

B= BY NOT

Rebelliousness is a negative form of action. There is a philosophy that you get what you give. If you resist, then what you get is resistance. In my own life, I know I've had to work harder and take a longer route toward my success because I fought the rules. I fought the rules of money, the rules of receiving an education, the rules of successful relationships and the rules of life. My resistance, my willingness to NOT play by the rules, resulted in many moments of frustration, anger, stress and resentment, as well as living in lack. I ended up feeling alone and isolated. When you take the negative action of resistance, the behaviors you exhibit may include: acting confused, defensive and isolating from others. In order to break yourself from the negative results of rebelliousness, you will have to take the first step by engaging with others.

E=ENGAGING

To engage is to connect, to be a part of, to be a piece of a bigger puzzle—life. In order to engage, you must break away from the rebel factor by reaching out to others and being vulnerable. You do this by letting others know you don't have to know how to do everything. You don't have to have the answers to everything to engage others. You do this by saying hello and being open to new and varied relationships. By engaging others, you are willing to be a part of a group—part of a successful group of people. Being a rebel creates the persona of a loner, someone who has chosen to stand apart, aloof and indifferent.

L=LEVERAGE

Leverage is using outside resources to assist you in following the rules and learning the rules.

This includes reaching out to others for support, building an effective network where you can offer your expertise and gain the expertise of others, and being willing to accept help from others who have been there before you (mentors, guides and teachers). It includes using the specialized knowledge found in libraries and support centers specifically created for your success (Small Business Administration centers, chambers of commerce, professional associations and universities). By using leverage you are also willing to be vulnerable in asking for help. Behaving like a rebel gives the impression you want to cause trouble and create chaos. Is that what you really want to do?

Rebelliousness worked for you when you were a toddler and a teen, as you broke through your dependence and moved toward independence. Now that you are an adult, the goal is interdependence: the ability to help each other be more prosperous, more successful, more loving and more connected. It's time to break through the rebelliousness and become a working member of successful teams in business, your home and life, by analyzing yourself and taking actions using the R.E.B.E.L. formula.

You're Entering the Discomfort Zone— But That's A Good Thing!

By Barbara Stanny

Whenever you decide to do something different—whether it's making money or losing weight—the desired result always lies just beyond reach, in the Discomfort Zone. The only way you'll get there is by stretching beyond what feels comfortable to do what may seem impossible, doing what you think you can't do.

While the first two steps in my Overcoming Underearning™ plan are meant to wake you up, this step demands you get out of bed, whether you feel like it or not. The stretch carries with it this strict stipulation: feel the fear, endure the discomfort, observe the resistance, and *go for it anyway*.

"We are taught that fear is something to avoid at all cost," Sally Beckett told me. "Since the workshop I've started listening to my gut. If it says 'You're afraid of this', I say 'That's a good thing. I'm going toward it. It'll force me to change and grow.'"

So how do you know when it's time to stretch? The signal to stretch comes in a variety of forms: you're assigned a project that feels out of your league; you're passed over for a promotion that was certainly yours; your new client sets an unreasonable deadline; a seeming coincidence sends you in a new direction; or a gut feeling says talk with your spouse, ask for a raise, or get out and network.

No matter how fervently that noisy voice in your head argues, or how nervous you feel, these opportunities—though they may feel more like ordeals—are the stepping stones that will take you to the next level.

But before you get there, you'll find yourself smack dab in the Discomfort Zone, an unpredictable passage where—maybe only for a moment, maybe for what seems like forever—your fate feels like a coin toss. You could succeed with a flourish or fall flat on your face. And you're forced to make a choice: Do I stay with what feels comfortable? Or do I go where I fear? If you opt for the latter, you'll probably want to zip through it as quickly as possible. But that's not the way it works. The Discomfort Zone has its own pace, and it's different for everyone. But keep in mind: the discomfort is short-lived, but the rewards can be life changing.

Meet Laurie, who started a business unpacking for people who have moved. She did a remarkable job of straightening out her finances because, she said "I forced myself to talk to a financial counselor and read every financial statement that came in the mail. I am a very results-oriented person. Once I decide to do something, I want it to be finished. I want to say: *Yes, I did it, it's done*. Unfortunately, you can't do that. You have to go through the process."

There's no escaping the Discomfort Zone. It's unsettling, filled with tension, and believe me, you'll be tested. You'll find yourself wavering, all set to forge ahead, but oh so tempted to stay where it's safe. Emotional vacillation is a common reaction when you're teetering on the brink, or in the full throes of a stretch.

Becky Corlis, an attractive single mom in her fifties, quit her job as a sales assistant in a financial firm to go into real estate—where, she said, "I could decide my value, not let someone else do it." When she gave her three weeks notice, her boss begged her to stay longer since she was going on vacation. Becky refused. Her boss was enraged.

"It was a stare-down, an actual stare-down," Becky recalled. "I just looked right back at her. There was one moment I was sure I was going to cave in. And before, I would have. I would've said 'Okay whatever you want. I am here to make your life easier,' thinking that was the more spiritual thing to do. Now I realize I have a voice. I don't have to be this mousy person stuck in a corner. So I said, 'This isn't convenient for me. I have given you enough time, and that's it.' This was her problem, not mine."

Then after a moment's pause in our interview, I watched the old Becky sneak back in as she added apologetically, "I sound so bad, don't I?"

"Why do you think that?" I asked, not surprised by the predictable relapse.

"It feels so heartless, and embarrassing," she stammered. Then hearing her words, she snapped back to her senses. "Wait! I'm not responsible for everyone else's happiness. That's a lie. They are grown up. They choose the way they want to be, and I get to choose what's right for me. It's not comfortable, it's scary, but that's okay. Afterwards, I actually felt wonderful."

I believe one of the major reasons people get stuck is because they're clinging to the very thing that's holding them in place. Nothing propels us into our Discomfort Zone quicker than letting go. And it's usually that which we're most afraid to let go of that is the very thing we need to release.

As Sally Beckett told me, "My biggest fear was losing my husband, so that's the fear I had to face. I had to be willing to walk away from him if he wasn't on the same path. So I gave him the ultimatum that we choose to be financially responsible and financially successful as a couple, or we can't be a couple, because the change was going to happen. I was no longer going to tolerate less pay for more work (his or mine), or this huge credit card debt, and if I was taking responsibility for making the changes with money, I had to make it across the board. Fortunately, he had the good sense to come with me."

The moral of Sally's story: You may not need to actually give anything up, but the willingness to do so frees you to take the necessary steps to reach the next level. It boils down to this: Do I let go of what's not serving me or do I abandon myself?

Adapted from *Overcoming Underearning™: A Five-Step Plan To A Richer Life*

Tame Your Shame: The Talking Cure

By Allison Acken, Ph.D.

Shame can stop us in our tracks faster than a speeding bullet. And money is an area ripe for shame, because shame is about secrets. Many of us have a secret about money—whether it's our spending, debt, assets, income, a big mistake or fear of the unknown. I certainly have had my secrets about money, although I have very few now, because I have found a cure: Start talking about it. Yes! Open your mouth and start talking about your money secrets. You'll be amazed at how liberating and enlightening it will be.

Have you ever had the experience of a friend saying she wants to tell you a horrible secret, but she's afraid you'll think less of her, or won't like her anymore? And when she tells you, you think, "This is a horrible secret?" We waste so much energy keeping secrets, when secrets are (mostly) best out in the open.

Two of my favorite stories from my work as a psychologist are about a wife with a huge secret debt, and a widow who was afraid to let her stockbroker know that she didn't understand him. In the first case, a woman, who was married to a loving, but commander-type husband, had accumulated $200,000 in debt over 20 years buying things he had vetoed. How he never noticed is beyond me, but he didn't. She was driving herself nuts with the anxiety and the pressure of hiding the bills, tucking away money, running for the bank statements before he could see them, and generally being terrified he would find out. She opened new credit card accounts and used cash advances to make payments on the old cards. Eventually, she maxed out, couldn't get more credit, and her house of cards was about to collapse.

After months of preparation, she invited her husband into her psychotherapy session so she could tell him her big secret. She was convinced he would divorce her. He launched right into talking about his work—the young men he managed and how he encouraged them to be financially sound. He advised them to review their credit reports each year for errors. I asked him if he had checked theirs lately. He replied, "No. Why?"

And then she told him. His first response was a prolonged silence. Then he said, "You must be paying $20,000 in interest alone each year. Is that why you have been so antsy lately? I thought you had a secret, but I was afraid you were having an affair." She sobbed with relief, and he immediately started figuring out how to shift money around to pay off the balances.

The secret that had taken over her life didn't end their marriage; in fact, it brought them closer. Of course, this was a basically strong marriage, and the fact that they had the funds available made the solution easier. But they would have made a plan even without "ready money," as the poet Shelley called it.

The second story is of a 76-year-old widow who whispered (literally!) that she didn't understand why her stockbroker suggested a particular financial strategy that week, but she didn't want to look stupid so she didn't say anything. This secret is not uncommon—too many financial advisors talk over the heads of their clients without realizing it. Clients are also hesitant to speak up, but the details here are priceless.

The widow's young broker had suggested she shift a significant amount of money into CDs. Her husband had been in the music business; she thought the broker meant to buy Compact Discs from the record store. She didn't think that was a very good investment move, but she was embarrassed to say so. She was considering changing brokers rather than having to confront him. Certificates of Deposit never occurred to her, until she said it out loud. Until she talked about it, she didn't have a clue. Secrets can keep us not only stuck, but also confused.

That's my money-talking cure. So what if you don't know everything, and you've made mistakes. Who hasn't? Talking provides us with comfort, clarity and choices. Secrets keep us stuck. Mind you, protect yourself at first. Pick your kindest friend or relative as your confidante—someone who is safe to talk to—not someone you know to be judgmental or negative. Once you start talking, you are, by definition, not stuck anymore.

Stuck On A story

By Betsy Deak

We all have stories accumulated throughout a lifetime of living. We learn them from parents, siblings, friends, school, partners, jobs, the world around us and the media. I define a "story" as a single incident that has been propped up by a succession of similar incidents. For example, if I lost money once as a child, my parents might have continued to remind me to be more careful, to keep track of my money and not to "lose it again." Whether I ever lose money again, this "story" can become the way I see myself: as someone who cannot handle or be trusted with money.

Holding onto these stories can feel safe and familiar. Yet each little story is like gum on my shoe—with each step I take, I unwittingly accumulate thoughts and beliefs that do not serve me and hinder my progress.

We all become very proficient in propping up these stories with any evidence we can find, most of which is faulty at best and paralyzing at worst. Many women never saw themselves as particularly athletic and now cannot imagine themselves running a marathon, rollerblading, kickboxing or enjoying a climbing gym. Some women haven't received a paycheck in so many years that they don't believe they are worthy of receiving money, while other women have lived a life of such scarcity that abundance seems sinful and/or for someone else.

We spend hours viewing ourselves in mirrors, yet very little time peering at what drives our inner thoughts.

Some useful questions are:

❂ How do I view myself?

❂ What "stories" surface when I think about facing any challenge?

❂ Is it a story that supports the best in me, or does it create a wall between where I am and where I want to go?

❂ Is this story preventing me from opening to new possibilities, people and my own potential?

A powerful exercise for becoming unstuck is to become aware of each "story" or "truth" that surfaces as you move through your day. Make an agreement with yourself to live for five minutes, a whole day, or even a week, as though no false stories, opinions or truths existed in your life.

As a strong opinion arises, ask the following questions:

❂ Is it true?

❂ How do I feel believing this?

❂ How does it serve me and those around me?

❂ What would my life be without that opinion?

There's a wonderful saying that goes: The only things we have to release to reach our dreams are the stories we tell ourselves about why we can't. Be open to the possibility that many of those stories create walls—not doorways—to unlimited potential for joy and abundance. Be ready to walk through those doors.

What Will You Do Today?

By Candace Bahr and Ginita Wall

We create our lives each day by choosing what we focus on. But too often what we focus on doesn't advance our lives or accomplish our goals. We are too caught up in our daily living to even figure out our goals, never mind taking steps to accomplish them.

Let us illustrate this with a story from our new book, *It's More Than Money—It's Your Life! The New Money Club for Women.*

On an outing to the beach, a grandmother decided to teach her granddaughter about the important things in life. She asked the girl to fill a pail with large rocks. Once the girl was finished, the grandmother asked her if the pail was full. "Oh, yes," said the girl, "I can't fit another rock in." Granny then told the girl to gather some small pebbles and put them into the pail. As she shook the pail lightly, her granddaughter saw how the pebbles rolled into the open areas between the rocks. The grandmother asked again if the pail was full. "Yes, of course, now it really is full," said her granddaughter.

Finally, the grandmother reached down for several handfuls of sand, which sifted through her fingers into the already-filled pail. "I guess the pail wasn't that full after all," said her granddaughter.

And so the grandmother taught her a valuable lesson she carried with her the rest of her life. When setting goals, take care of the rocks first—the important things in your life. If you fill your pail with sand, the small stuff, there is no room for anything else.

What are the large rocks in your life? They are probably the things that are most important—your family, your health, your spiritual life, your security. The pebbles are the other things that matter such as your job, your house, or your car. The sand is everything else—the small stuff. If you spend all your energy and time on the small stuff, you will never have room for the things that matter most. Take care of the rocks. Set your priorities. The rest is just sand.

Celebrate new beginnings

This is the perfect time to set the course for the rest of your life. Here's how to do it. Take a pen and paper and spend 15 minutes writing down what is important to you and where you are going. What do you want your life to become? What can you do to get there? Open yourself to the possibilities, and create a vision of a future filled with abundance. It's time to go forward without dwelling on the past. Whatever has happened in your life, wherever you are today, it's time to celebrate new beginnings.

You can have anything in your life you want. What do you want? That's a tough one, isn't it? Let your imagination run wild, and write down everything that comes to mind. Pretend you have met a genie with a magic wand who will grant you anything you want. Once you've listed all the possibilities, review them and discard the ones that don't seem that important. Make a list of your important goals. As you write your list, don't hold back—there is no need to determine *how* you're going to get everything on the list just yet.

Fill your life with ROCKS

Use the ROCKS method to turn your dreams into goals. Your goals do need to be real and focused, so you can commit your energy to reaching them. The word "ROCKS" is an acronym that can help you remember the key elements you need to make your vision of a new life come true.

Realistic. Do you have the time and skills to achieve your goals? If they seem too lofty, don't abandon them. Just break them down into small steps, and do the steps one at a time.

Obtainable. You must believe in your goal. Remember, if you believe it, you can achieve it.

Controllable. Your goal must be something that is within your power to do, not something that is dependent on outside forces.

Keep trying. If things don't go as you planned, revise your plans so you can achieve what you set out to do.

Specific. Write down your goals. Use as many concrete and specific terms as you can to describe your goals, and when you intend to reach them.

Goals vs. dreams

Congratulations! You have now completed an important step that most people fail to do. Less than 1 percent of Americans write down specific goals each year. Writing down your goals is powerful. More than 50 years ago Harvard University polled a class of graduates. Fewer than 3 percent of them had written goals. When Harvard polled them again 20 years later, that small 3 percent had become wealthier than the rest of the class combined! Not only that, but they were also healthier and more content. That's the power of writing down your goals.

You may have heard about this study, and wondered how it could be true. We can't tell you the exact process, but we have seen the power of this in our own lives. Seventeen years ago, when Ginita wrote down that she wanted to be an author, she hadn't even written one book. Our new book, *It's More Than Money—It's Your Life*, is now her eighth book. Candace and her husband John create a collage each year to help them visualize what they would like to accomplish in seven areas of their lives. As they review the previous year's collage each January, it's amazing how closely their life accomplishments track the collage. Even their teenage daughter Carrie puts together a collage each year with things that are significant in her life.

Small steps lead to big success

As you have seen, the first step in achieving your goals is to visualize the goal and believe you can reach it. The next step is to write it down, as specifically as possible. And of course you have to follow up with action that will make those goals a reality.

Sometimes we think we have to make major changes in our lives to get ourselves on track. But in reality, major changes are the result of a series of small steps. Step by step, day by day, you can change your life. Decide how you will take action toward your financial dreams. What small steps are you going to take to move your life forward? What will you do today?

We so strongly believe in the concept of Small Steps that we've made it the focal point of our new Money Club web site. At the web site, each day you'll find three examples of Small Steps you can do in 15 minutes or less to accomplish your financial goals. Just take one small step every day, and you can change your financial life forever. Remember: It's more than money — it's your life!

Something I'm Grateful For Is. . .

By Marci Shimoff

I was in a funk—a big funk—and it was going on too long! It was September 1987, and a few months earlier I had broken up with my boyfriend, Bob, a wonderful man whom I loved and respected, but who I just didn't feel was "the one." So rather than drag things on any longer, I decided it was time for us to move on and be open to our respective life partners. We'd enjoyed a deep and sweet relationship together for two years, so breaking up wasn't easy, but for the first few weeks, I was fine.

Then he met ***her***, another woman. He started dating Holly and very soon they were in love. To make matters worse she was a friend of mine who lived just around the corner. Every time I drove home, I could see his car outside her house. Somehow, while I didn't want to be with him, I certainly didn't want anyone else to be with him either. Selfish, of course, but it seemed I couldn't help but feel that way. Every feeling of hurt, betrayal and abandonment came to the surface and I overreacted. I was in deep pain, and I felt even worse for feeling so bad. I knew I should feel happy for them and just move on, but I felt trapped by my pain.

Every friend under the sun heard about it. My therapist heard about it. . .over and over again. It was coloring my work, my life. The only good news was that I lost those ten pounds I'd been wanting to lose for years, and I was fitting into my tight jeans (I call it the break-up diet). But that offered only slight consolation.

After three months of this, my friends were tired of hearing about it. And I was tired of feeling it, but nothing was lifting. I was stuck.

Then one morning, Holly showed up at my door and asked to come in and talk with me. She knew what I was going through and wanted to help. So after sharing her own stories of post break-up woes, she said it to me straight.

"Marci, you're in a funk, and you've got to get out of it. It's time. You're only looking at what's not working in your life. You're forgetting all the great things that you've got. You've got to turn this around. So I want you to promise me that you'll do what I'm going to tell you." I was desperate, so I agreed to do whatever she was going to advise.

She continued. "Every night before you go to sleep, I want you to write down five things you are grateful for from that day. You must write them down. And I want you to do it for 21 days straight." (Psychologists often say it takes 21 days to change a habit.) I agreed. How hard could this be?

Well, it was hard. The first few days I really had to stretch. I didn't want to focus on what was good in my life. It was much easier to complain. I ended up with things on the list like *I'm grateful that I had lunch today*. As the days went on, they got deeper: *I'm grateful for my great friends* and *I'm grateful for my good health.* Remarkably, by the 21st day, my funk had lifted. It was true that I had so much to be grateful for, and I not been focusing on any of that.

My life turned around. In fact, this simple little exercise worked so well that I continued doing it every night for the next three years. Even today, when I start to get into a funk, I go back to my reliable gratitude exercise and it always helps me regain perspective.

During that same conversation with Holly, we decided to form a women's support group together. Along with five other women, we met once a week to share with each other our wins or successes from the previous week and our intentions for the upcoming week. We met for over ten years, and we saw each other through many life events: marriages (Bob and Holly), children, deaths. Our support group became our family.

I eventually moved away, but recently hosted Bob and Holly and their teenage daughter to a week at my home in the San Francisco area. We had a wonderful time together, and I consider them my dear, dear friends.

Now whenever I am stuck in my life, I focus on the two gifts Holly brought to me that September day in 1987: gratitude and support.

Top two tips for breaking through:

1. For the next 21 days, every night before you go to sleep, write down five things you are grateful for that day. Once you get through those 21 days, you'll see how you want to keep this simple but powerful exercise going. What you put your attention on grows stronger in your life. You'll see how much more will show up in your life that you can feel grateful for.

2. Form a support team. Find a group of like-minded women (I love women's support groups, though I'm sure mixed groups are wonderful too), and meet regularly. Share your wins from the previous week and your intentions for the upcoming week. There's great wisdom in the expression that we have to live our lives ourselves, but we don't have to do it alone.

The Perfect Life Pause

By Katana Abbott

I have found a wonderful solution to help create balance in my life and it only takes three minutes. I call this process The Perfect Life Pause. Anytime during the day that I feel overwhelmed, stressed, tired or angry, I follow this process to refocus my energy and intention.

Many American women are really on an adrenaline rush all the time. I've found if we don't slow down and allow things to flow, the Universe finds a way to do it for us.

I suggest doing your first Perfect Life Pause when you first wake up. Start with your eyes closed. Listen to the sounds in the room, your breathing… notice your body and relax. Then focus on what you would wish for in your life if you had a magic wand and could manifest any wish you wanted. This would be your Perfect Life. Focus on how you would feel, what you would be doing and how you would look.

Now spend the next several minutes in this wonderful state of mind believing it is real. At the end of the three minutes, be sure to express gratitude and believe this will be your Perfect Life. Confirm that the right people and opportunities will flow into your life at the right time.

By doing this exercise three to four times a day, you will actually be meditating and focusing on your intentions a total of 10-15 minutes each day. Remember, we get what we focus on! Each day we create our reality through our thoughts…and we are all very intricately connected somehow.

Let me give you an example. My husband, Mark, and I were in San Francisco last August for a conference. Prior to the conference, we went to Napa for a wine tasting experience. It was one of the best vacations we ever had. We spent three days driving through wine country in a convertible surrounded by azure skies and the most beautiful scenery we had ever seen.

During our trip, we purchased several cases of wonderful wine and brought them back to our hotel in San Francisco, thinking we'd find some packing tape and just ship the wine back with our luggage. We were enjoying our trip so much that we never really looked seriously for the tape.
We had an early flight back to Detroit and were ready to take our bags down for the trip to the airport, when we realized we still didn't have any packing tape. I called the front desk, and they said all they had was scotch tape.

I told Mark I was going to go downstairs and find some tape. Specifically, I said, "Let's create the intention that we'll find some packing tape and send that intention out to the Universe to see what happens." He looked at me and said, "Let's do it!" So we left the hotel room and stepped into the elevator.

There was another couple in the elevator from our group, and I noticed they were holding a box, so I said, "What's in the box, did you buy wine too? We're trying to find some packing tape." The man said, "No, these are our costumes. We never even opened the box, and we still have our packing tape." The woman looked at me and said, "Do you need some tape? Here take it—we never used it."

And she opened her backpack and handed me a roll of packing tape. At that moment the elevator door opened up and they stepped out.

We said goodbye and pushed the button to go back to our floor. We were both speechless. We ran back to our hotel room, slammed the door and screamed with amazement!

How does something like that happen? Some may say it's just a coincidence. I say we created an intention and it materialized. I now do this all the time…it's amazing once you become aware of this principle. I keep the empty tape dispenser in my dresser as a reminder.

To do this exercise correctly, you'll need to create goals by writing them down and then placing them where you can read them every day. This is the principle behind focusing on your Perfect Life Pause. Something happens when you focus on your goals…you actually materialize what you want. That's why I also recommend making your goals Big and Bold, writing them in present tense and then focusing on your Perfect Life Pause several times a day.

Go For Your Best Case Scenario

By Elizabeth P. Anderson

Here's a simple, yet powerful two-part exercise. First, ask yourself: What's the **worst** thing that could happen to me if I: ask for a raise / invite a man I'm attracted to out to the theater / call up that prospect / whatever?

Write down all the possible negative consequences you can think of. Most of them will probably boil down to some form of *I'll be no better or worse off than I already am.* My boss will tell me it's too soon for a raise, or the man won't be interested, or the prospect will hang up on me and I won't make a sale. Notice how this makes you feel.

Then visualize the **best** thing that could happen. See yourself getting whatever it is you want: the raise, the client, the contract, the new friend. Rehearse in your mind what you have to do or say to get it. Really let yourself experience in your visualization the way you'll feel when you achieve your goal: the pride, the relief from stress, the joy, whatever feeling you desire.

Next, mentally weigh the two feelings against each other. Very often this will lead to a go-for-it attitude, because you'll realize that if you're willing to risk just a temporary bit of disappointment or embarrassment, you'll open up enormous opportunities.

(Then again, maybe you'll dissuade yourself. Maybe you don't *really* want to try parachuting, after all.)

Give Yourself A Sensory Experience

By Oriana Green

Has getting mentally stuck caused you to become physically inactive? Are you feeling inert, rock-like? Most of us have those times when we just don't want to get out of bed, and when we certainly don't want to tackle the project that has us stymied.

My solution for this does require a leap—or perhaps just a step—of faith that it will work. Even though it's the last thing you want to do, it's the first thing you need to do. Get up, put on your walking shoes and get out of the house. Make yourself go for a walking meditation of at least 20 minutes. Longer is even better.

This is very different from a social stroll with a friend or a jaunt to the corner for coffee. This is an intentional walk, where you actively engage all your senses to reinvigorate them. By stimulating your heart and large muscle groups, you can't help but feel a bit more alive.

Walk somewhere you don't usually go, or walk your regular route in the opposite direction. Force yourself to notice things you haven't seen before. Really look at your environment. Let your gaze be drawn to colors you love. Notice where that pulls your thoughts.

Listen to the sounds in your world. Is there music drifting from a window? Is someone's cat on the prowl? Do you hear the wind? What memories do these sounds evoke?

What smells do you encounter on your walk? Do you pass a bakery? Has a neighbor just cut her lawn? What scent does the breeze carry? Try and smell something you never have—the bark of a tree, a stone, a fence. Reach down to the earth and smell fresh dirt.

Now engage your sense of touch. Again, seek things you wouldn't normally touch—the woven pattern of wire in a gate, wisps of ornamental grasses, the texture of stepping stones, a worm.

Finally, taste something. A leaf, a pansy, dew on the grass—or yes, you can finish up at a café—as long as you order something new and different. Try and figure out all the ingredients that went into what you're eating or drinking. Where were they grown? Imagine what raw wheat would taste like, or an unroasted coffee bean.

If you really commit to this process, you'll soon get lost in the pure fun of it and tap into that precious, untainted perception of a child for whom everything is new. The real payoff comes as you examine your project in this new state of sensory stimulation. Look at it from another angle, backwards or upside down! Since what you've been doing wasn't working, ask yourself what you can do differently. If you are patient with yourself, new ideas and approaches will appear.

So the next time you feel like pulling the covers over your head, instead go outside and smell the rain. Or the snow. Or a pine cone.

Stop Fixing: Use Intuitive Intelligence Instead

By Nancy Rosanoff

When my youngest daughter was 17, I saw her driving around town with her friends, smoking. She saw that I saw; something she had been hiding was now revealed. Smoking was forbidden in our house, the one unacceptable behavior my husband and I had been completely clear on.

Ways to fix the problem were lining up in my mind: taking away privileges, grounding, screaming and yelling about "how could she do this to us?"

Fortunately for us all, intuitive intelligence prevailed when I took a deep breath and realized there was nothing to fix. I knew if I looked at this as a *situation* rather than as a problem, I would find a positive way to engage it.

The only real problem was that I wasn't getting what I wanted—she was behaving in ways that I did not approve of. When I thought of punishing her, I realized, I felt nothing but tension—intuitive resistance. So instead, I asked her some questions, which felt much more comfortable. How did she feel about it? How did she want to handle telling her father? She said she'd been thinking about quitting for the last few weeks, and now she was sure she would. I conveyed to her that while smoking was forbidden, I was not about to stop loving her, and I was pleased she wanted to quit and would support her in any way I could.

The problem healed itself; within a month she had stopped smoking. Had I focused on solving the problem by attempting to change or fix her behavior, the chances are she would have resisted and resented my well-intentioned actions. As it turned out, the fact that I saw her smoking was a wake-up call for her to quit on her own.

Intuitive intelligence tells us not to attempt to fix things. The intuitive approach is to realize that whatever is happening, good or bad, can be seen as information. Pay attention to the information instead of to your emotional response to the situation, and the solution will come to you.

Here are some guidelines for responding when faced with a situation that seems like a problem:

❂ Recognize that at its core, what makes the situation a problem is that what is happening is not what you want to happen. Focusing on the problem and attempting to fix it will limit your ability to see the opportunities your intuitive intelligence is gathering.

❂ Instead of doing something about the situation, take a breath and open your mind to new perspectives and information, details that were previously overlooked or minimized.

❂ Become aware of which possible actions give you a sense of tension and which give a sense of ease. Move in the direction of ease.

❂ Let the situation move itself. As you take a pause in the activity involved with the situation, some synchronistic information or opportunity might appear, or the appropriate direction will come as an inspiration. Remember that even though you may have stopped taking action, your intuitive intelligence is always active and in touch with all possible solutions.

What To Do in the Middle of the Night When You Are Anxious

By Carol Adrienne, Ph.D.

During a period of flux or imminent loss, you may go in and out of agitation, fear, worry and catastrophic thinking. ("If I lose this job, I could be out of work for years!" or "If my boyfriend breaks up with me, I don't think I could take it" or "If something doesn't happen soon, I could be out on the street.")

There are days when you feel you can cope, but there also may be nights that flood you with fear, so here are some suggestions for those times.

Create a gratitude mantra

Since you can't think yourself out of your problems, let go of trying to control things that are out of your control. Train yourself to go to gratitude. Begin repeating a prayer that goes something like this: "Thank you for all that I have received. Thank you for: (specific things like good health, family members, friends, your work or home, the bed you are sleeping on, the pillow, the clean water in the tap, the hot shower that you will take, and so on)."

You get the point. By being thankful for everything, you put yourself in a more harmonious vibration—the vibration of love, humility and receptivity. The vibration of gratitude is a powerful healer and energy releaser.

Be still

During the night, lie peacefully on your back, and follow your breath in and out. Cultivate an inner stillness. As thoughts come through, let them drift on by. Try not to figure out anything. Remind yourself that everything that has happened and is happening is strengthening you. Your experiences are in some way necessary in order for you to learn, accept or change a situation that you have perhaps outgrown. Notice anyone who pops into your mind. How might this person have a piece of wisdom for you?

Send out love

As you lie in the dark, send out loving energy to all the people who might be thinking of you or remembering you—all the people who saw you during the day, who have ever met you, and who may meet you in the future. Positive feelings open you up energetically.

Pre-pave the future

If you are lying awake because of anxiety about a meeting or task ahead, imagine yourself in the scenario. Fill your scene with radiant light. See yourself succeeding and receiving the rewards and results you desire and deserve. See yourself smiling, shaking hands, having people listening to you, nodding their heads or opening the door into a scene you want to live in. Notice that everyone in the scene is receiving his or her highest good at that moment as well. Thank God and All That Is for helping you to accomplish future tasks with effortless ease. Spend only a couple of minutes on this visualization. When the energy feels complete, let your vision go and go back to sleep. Tell yourself that all is well.

Expect effortless connections to helpful people

In the morning before you arise, remember to say, "Today I want to meet good people." During the day, look for people who seem to be on your wavelength. As you use your affirmation to attract new people with whom you resonate, take the time to get to know them, invite them for tea or a walk. Spend less time with negative people who drain your energy or who amplify your own fears ("Jobs are scarce" or "Men always leave you for someone else.")

A woman named Lucy had been laid off three times in five years from administrative jobs. Seeking the purpose of these upsets, she asked herself what she really enjoyed doing, which turned out to be playing the piano—seemingly unrelated to employment. A couple of weeks went by. She happened to go to a local mall, where she noticed a new music store. She went in. After a brief conversation with a clerk who wasn't able to answer her questions about a keyboard, she was about to leave when he brought over the manager. Another conversation ensued.

This time the manager was so impressed with Lucy's questions that she offered her a job as a saleswoman! Lucy, who had never worked in sales, modestly dismissed the idea, saying she had no experience. The manager replied, "Oh, we'd rather you not have experience, because our customers don't like to feel pressured by a professional sales pitch." Lucy took this unexpected opportunity and is now very happy with her job.

Refresh your energy and eliminate drains

During the day, it's critical to get some exercise, so be sure to include something enjoyable like walking or yoga as a necessary part of your schedule. Regaining balance and maintaining it is not necessarily accomplished by some brilliant idea that you come up with that solves all your problems. Balance, fulfillment and security are built on everyday decisions to take care of yourself each day as best you can, in an ongoing commitment to move forward. If you can, be sure to make room for fun activities. Light-heartedness magnetizes good things.

When You Go to the Well, Bring A Bucket

By Kellie Carbone

Recently, I was sitting with Heidi, who told me she was feeling stuck and confused about what she should do with her life. She had several ideas and interests, but none seemed to stand out as the path she should take. She's passionate about pottery, languages and the healing arts, but she was struggling to figure out how they might blend together into a work life that would feel meaningful and important.

Her mother was pressuring her to get a "real job," and her boyfriend was reluctant to commit to her unless she was bringing in a steady income. It seemed everyone had an opinion about what she should do, and they were more than happy to share their thoughts with her.

As Heidi spoke, I could feel her anxiety rise as her mind raced to find a solution. She looked at me, desperate for an answer. In that moment, I asked her one simple question: "Do you meditate?"

My best piece of advice on how to overcome blocks and create the life you dream of, is that you must spend at least 30 minutes every day in quiet time or meditation.

Through my personal and professional experiences, I believe all blocks to success result from feeling disconnected from the universal creative flow that is ever available to us. When we get quiet, we can release the noise and interruption of the world around us. It is in the midst of this quiet space that we can begin to hear our own voice. Paramahansa Yogananda stated that if you don't meditate, "the whole world will crowd in to claim you."

Imagine someone telling you they are thirsty and in need of water. You tell them you know of a well where the water is pure and abundant, and they can go there whenever they need to receive their fill. What would you think if you saw this person show up at this rich supply to collect water with a colander?

The image may seem ridiculous, but I have found that many of us do the same thing when it comes to seeking inspiration and guidance on our paths. The universe is an endless pool from which we can fill ourselves, and yet we rarely show up at its edge prepared to take the nourishment we seek. Meditation is the container into which we receive inspiration and clarity.

When Heidi began to meditate, she discovered that doing her art and being with children were the two most important things in her life. Each day, she would sit quietly and listen to her inner sense of knowing about the situation. Within a few weeks, she felt clear that she wanted to open her own art studio where children could come to explore their creativity. She is now in the process of creating a business plan and looking for investors.

We all have a purpose in life, a set of gifts that we are meant to share with the world. Meditating drops us down to a place within ourselves where all other concerns can fall away. We can release ourselves from the voices and expectations of others and begin to hear what's inside our hearts. When we are quiet, we begin to receive guidance and certainty about the direction our lives should take. Our desires and gifts are revealed, along with the action needed to manifest our dreams. Once we tap into what it is that we most want to share with the world, there is little that can stop us.

Some tips for a rewarding meditation practice

❂ Settle quietly into your thoughts and ask for guidance. Some people may call this source of guidance "god" or "goddess;" some may call it earth, spirit, intuition or instinct. ***It does not matter what you call it, it only matters that you call upon it.***

❂ There is no right or wrong way to meditate. You can sit quietly, paying attention to your breath or your mind's tendency to wander. You can follow a guided visualization. Others begin each meditation session with a question in mind, such as: "What is it that I need to pay attention to as I make this decision?" Find what works for you, and make a commitment to do it every day.

❂ Set aside a space in your home where you can meditate. It can be a spare room, a closet or simply a corner designated for your quiet time. Consider decorating this area with pillows, plants, colorful fabric or candles. Create a space you look forward to visiting.

❂ If you're struggling with making an important decision, or if you are experiencing conflict in a relationship, contemplate the matter in your meditation time. By connecting with this resource, you will gain clarity and a better understanding of any necessary action.

❂ Keep a journal. Just as you would not show up to the well empty handed, be prepared to collect the ideas and inspiration you receive during your meditation time. Writing down your ideas makes them real and sends a message to the universe that you are ready to receive more.

❂ Protect your meditation time. Turn off the phone and close the door behind you. It may require that you wake before the rest of your family so you won't be interrupted. Do what you must to carve out this time. If you commit to this practice, the rewards will be immeasurable.

What's Next?

By Vanessa Wesley

This may be one of the most powerful questions to ask when you are feeling stuck. Many of us do use several of the tools of goal-setting, visualizing, networking and so forth in order to actualize what it is we desire. In fact, numerous women have a very clear plan of the action steps needed to reach their goals. But what often happens is that we become overwhelmed with the planning and the need to have control over the various outcomes. We find the planning can be a struggle and frequently our plans fall through, forcing us to redesign them once again. If this sounds like you, here's an idea. STOP!

Breathe. Connect in. The creative source of who you are is not "outside" in the plans and activity—it is within.

Place your attention on your solar plexus, the area below your ribcage. Breathe. Go inside. Now bring to mind your goal, the highest vision you have for yourself. Take your time and use all of your senses. What does it look like? Where are you? What sounds do you hear? What tastes? Get a very specific and clear vision on what you want to manifest.

You are not attempting to figure anything out such as *how* you are going to achieve the goal, or even *when*. Simply sit with the highest vision for yourself, the end result.

While holding your vision clearly in mind go to that inner place at the solar plexus and ask your inner wisdom, that intuitive place that resides in you, What's next?

Breathe. Allow an answer to bubble up. It is not necessary to make one up. Here's when it gets fun! Go with the answer. It may have been as mundane as Do the dishes, or as surprising as Go to the library. Or it may have come to you not in words, but as an energy that urges you to do gardening, or to begin cooking dinner, or to make a phone call to someone you haven't talked to in a long time. Follow it. Amazing things happen when you follow this guidance. Using creative guidance is not linear. What bubbles up inside you to do next may not make rational sense. That's the adventure.

Practice asking, What's next? each step of the way, perhaps in the morning before the day gets started for you, and whenever you don't know what to do next. As you follow this inner guidance, you will begin to notice wonderful synchronicities opening up for you—chance meetings and information seeming to come out of the blue.

This doesn't take the place of strategic planning and focusing on practical action steps. What it does is get you unstuck. It moves you and energizes you. In essence it allows you to get yourself, your rational thinking mind, out of your way. With continued practice you will make the right moves and be at the right place at the right time. This is truly a delightful experience. When you become soul-directed, you will achieve your goals in ways you could not have planned, and your life will take on an energized aliveness.

Open Your Hands

By Sharon J. Anderson

Often we remain stuck because we refuse to let go. We hold tight to mistaken judgments about our gifts and skills because, more often than not, these judgments feel familiar and comfortable. But like bacteria, these judgments can erode our mental health and deplete our spiritual strength. Sometimes we simply have to let go.

I learned this lesson in a vivid way the day I visited Shanksville, Pennsylvania following the premiere of a short documentary video I had directed about 9/11 first responders. One of the first responders featured in the video was Corporal Craig Bowman, the Pennsylvania state trooper in charge of the United Flight 93 crime scene, who had invited me to Shanksville. Throughout our visit, even while answering my questions while standing at the impact site, Corporal Bowman remained unflappable. His answers were short and succinct: "No ma'am. Yes, ma'am."

Finally I asked him if he had ever lost his composure during 9/11 and its aftermath. He replied, "Yes." It happened the day family members came to view the debris field. Unable to see their faces behind the tinted windows of their transport buses, but wanting to reach out to them, Corporal Bowman simply saluted as the buses passed by. From the inside, a sea of open hands instantaneously appeared, pressed against the bus windows.

"They were reaching out to me despite their loss," said Bowman. "I'll never forget it. I try now to live my life with open hands and not clenched fists."

The next time you find yourself stuck because your fists are clenched tightly around your mistakes, shortcomings or losses, let go. Literally open your hands. Reach out. Live your life.

Eight Ways To Overcome Sabotaging Behaviors

by Marcia Wieder

Here are the most common ways we sabotage our dreams and happiness and suggestions for trying something else.

⊛ **SABOTAGE #1:** Negative self-talk and self-doubt are useless. This is the art of telling yourself all the things that are wrong with you and/or your idea, and all the reasons why you can't have what you want. This is the voice of your critic, and for many of us this can be a very loud voice.

SUGGESTION: Your thoughts create your reality. Change your mind, as well as what you are actually saying, and you will change your reality. Design one core belief, that if you believed it, would help you move forward on your dream. For one week, practice believing this new belief—especially when you hear your self-doubt shouting at you. Change your beliefs, change your thoughts and you will change your reality.

⊛ **SABOTAGE #2:** Putting your fears into your dream will kill the dream. Fear is part of your present reality. Here and now, you may have fear or doubt about your dream, but by projecting that fear into the dream, you are sabotaging any possibility you have of moving forward. If you are using "what if" thinking, you are creating a false barrier.

SUGGESTION: Any fears you have about your dreams are just part of the present reality.

Divide a piece of paper in half. Label the top "My Dream" and the bottom half "My Reality." Honestly describe the dream and then assess your reality about the dream. Include in the reality section all of your fears about the dream. Now you can clearly see where you stand. You can also decide (on a daily basis) if you are more committed to your dream or to your reality, which includes your fears.

❂ **SABOTAGE #3:** Being vague about the dream will keep you confused. If you don't have clarity about your dream, it's difficult to know what to do about it or to ask anyone for help. Successful dreamers have learned to articulate their vision in a way that gets others excited and on board, an impossibility without clarity.

SUGGESTION: Speaking powerfully about your dreams is essential for establishing credibility with yourself as well as with others. Practice writing your dream down and speaking it out loud. This type of clarity will help you explore your thoughts and feelings about your dreams, as well as bring up any limiting beliefs and fears that need to be identified, explored and resolved.

❂ **SABOTAGE #4:** If the dream stays a dream, it will not become a reality. Dreaming is a wonderful place to start, but unless you are interested in living a fantasy life, it's essential that the dream be moved forward. A big dream cannot be put on a "to do" list. It needs to be broken down into more manageable steps.

SUGGESTION: Break the dream into small, easily accomplishable, short-term projects. A project, like a goal, must have a completion date. Next, break the project into single items to do and schedule them into your life (by putting them on your calendar). Now most importantly, do something every day or at least every week to accomplish your project. By accomplishing your projects, you will accomplish your dreams.

SABOTAGE #5: Scheduling unrealistic deadlines will lead to disappointment. And disappointment can cause you to give up or not to be able to see new opportunities or other solutions. If you overwhelm yourself, all kinds of strange and unnecessary things may happen.

SUGGESTION: Take the project one step at a time. Look at what else is happening in your life and learn to schedule creatively and efficiently. Use your time wisely. Be clear about what the specific tactics or items to do are, and try to realistically estimate how long it will take to get each one done. Set up a simple system so you can see you are making progress. If you keep doing the things necessary to get the project done, it will happen. Just keep going.

✪ **SABOTAGE #6:** Loss of perspective can send you into a tailspin. Telling yourself that you will never make it, or how bad things are, is a sure way to sabotage your dream. If you don't know where you are, how can you make clear decisions on strategy or know where to go to get help? Not telling yourself the truth can be harmful to you and your dream.

SUGGESTION: Practice reporting accurately on where you are and the status of your dream. Keep checking in on your feelings and your intention, and notice where you are stuck or stopped. Conversely, reward yourself and celebrate when you achieve a milestone. Create measurement tools or visual displays so you can see at any given moment where you are. This helps you save time, use your resources better and keeps you honest and motivated.

❂ **SABOTAGE #7:** Don't get caught believing "It's so much easier to do it myself." As busy as you are, if there's an easier way to make your dream happen, don't you want to know about it? Are you sabotaging your dream by declaring you are the only one who can do all the things it will take to get the job done, while complaining you just don't have the time to do them, so therefore nothing is happening?

SUGGESTION: Get help. Identify the resources that are at your fingertips or a phone call away and start to use them. Ideally, build a Dream Circle or at least identify one person who will support you on making this dream actually happen. It could be a great buddy or spouse who will support you by holding you accountable for doing the things you said you would do. The single most powerful thing you can do to make your dream come true is share your dream with someone who is on your side.

❂ **SABOTAGE #8**: If you kill yourself in the process, you won't get to enjoy the dream. The worst thing that could possibly happen is you forget about you. If you sell out on your own well-being in order to make the dream happen, surely you will suffer and probably so will the dream.

SUGGESTION: Your well being needs to be taken care of, so you will have extra energy to take care of others and all the details. This is a critical point. If you are not calm and centered, there is little chance your dream will flourish. Along the path to your dream, take care of your body, mind, heart and soul, and you will deliver unto this world your heart's desire.

Are You Stuck with Negative Money Associations?

By Shell Tain

If you are experiencing anything less than unlimited abundance, then you might be stuck in your thinking about money. I've found it can help to become aware of and monitor your language when you think or talk about money. See if you have a bingo moment as you consider the monetary associations that follow.

We all know money is actually a symbol, a concept given form. But do you really realize how pervasive that symbol is? The concept of money was originally constructed as a bartering symbol: I give you money so I can buy your goat, rather than having to exchange my wheat for the goat, since you really don't want the wheat.

A great example of how things might have worked before money was amusingly portrayed in several episodes of M*A*S*H, where Radar worked the system exchanging all sorts of odd things to end up with what he really wanted. Money theoretically simplifies all that. But at what price (pun intended)?

Even though we have paper and metal tokens to represent money, it really is just a concept, not an actual item. Yet we seem to have taken the concept to other and unintended extremes. We assign meaning and significance to money that is purely arbitrary, and we sometimes act as if money had its own volition. We even blame things on money when we believe ideas such as: "Rich people aren't as nice as poor people" or "I always struggle with money." These statements imply that money itself is the responsible party, rather than the humans involved.

There are many words in our culture which relate to both money and our sense of who we are. Let's examine a few:

❂ **Worth and worthy.** Notice how often we seem to tie our worthiness to our net worth. We even speak of "self-worth."

❂ **Value and values.** Things have value. Money has value. People act on their values. What do you value?

❂ **Trust.** How does the concept of being trustworthy tie to the concept of setting up a trust to safeguard your assets?

❂ **Spend.** I spend money. I also spend time. Are there connections between how you consume your money and your time?

❂ **Credit.** We use the word "credit" to imply validity and trustworthiness, even to give praise. And of course we also refer to "credit" as how much money we can borrow. Do you have any mental associations between the number of credit cards you have and how good you feel about yourself? How about your credit limit?

❂ **Save.** This was the first money metaphor I came across in my life. As a child I had heard about how "Jesus Saves." There was a building downtown that had huge red neon lights above it spelling out "Jesus Saves." As a five-year-old kid I decided this sign was over a bank, and that this bank was so good, even Jesus saved there. Seemed perfectly logical to me. How does the idea of soul saving and money saving co-mingle in your mind? Is there some judgment about how much better a person you might be if you saved more?

❂ **Broke.** Here's the big one—if you are broke are you broken? Many people feel a direct connection here, as if being broke makes you broken. Conversely, do you believe money fixes things?

As humans we are pattern makers, and in that vein we are also metaphorical thinkers. In many areas this can be a valuable and effective tool. But when it comes to money, the metaphors and homonyms can exacerbate the situation rather than simplify it.

Spend some time exploring where you associate money words and concepts with other aspects of your life. In order to change the money path your mind takes, you first have to acknowledge all the twists and turns you have already been down.

Ask Yourself Some Tough Questions

By Jody Jungerberg

In 2002 I completed the coursework for my MBA. For a divorced mom with two teenaged daughters, it was a long grind of night school while working full-time and keeping my family together. My studies were made even more difficult, because I was nearing the end of a year in a job I hated. But a class in leadership that last semester turned my life around and helped me get unstuck from a situation that was increasingly intolerable.

The first assignment given to the class was to find out what kind of leader we wanted to be by asking:

- What are our core values?
- What is our personal mission on this earth?
- Whom do we love most in this world?

The rationale for teaching this in a business course was simple yet complex: You will bring your core self into your company, and you must know exactly what you stand for and who you are. You must have a clear definition of what you value and what your priorities are—personally and professionally. Once you know these answers, decisions become easier and less gray. Those who work with you will sense your strength and heed your guidance much more than they would take direction from someone who bullies, threatens and manipulates others.

Focusing on my values eventually led me to face that I was working in a company culture that was the opposite of what I knew I stood for. I was encouraged to sell products that would produce the most commission, even if it wasn't in the best interest of my clients. I was living a lie, in a job that was toxic to my soul. How could I become a values-based leader if I was working in an environment that was not compatible with my core values? I was suffering a moral dilemma. But I felt trapped by the economic necessity of having to support my family. I couldn't just quit.

I needed to find a way to assist my clients with honesty and integrity. I consulted friends and family, I networked, sent out resumes and did all I could to stop the behavior at work that made me so uncomfortable. My paycheck slipped accordingly, but I was sleeping better, even though I labeled myself a professional failure.

And then I wrote down my definition of success (which had nothing to do with a title or money, and had everything to do with valuing what my soul told me to value). After that exercise, things began to improve. It was as if the universe was listening and bringing me the positive energy I needed to move forward. In my leadership class I learned I was not alone in this type of struggle.

We all researched great leaders, and we all did presentations in front of each other in class. This sharing at least gave me the confidence to know I would eventually get past the internal struggle. Shortly after I finished that class, a corporate recruiter contacted me, and I soon joined an organization that I believed I could thrive in. The silver lining was finally showing.

The route to a life lived with integrity is self-examination and aligning your actions with your values. Listen to the quiet voice inside, and it will guide you home.

Writer, Producer, Star!

By Rosemary Davies-Janes

Perhaps you are feeling stuck because you're acting out the wrong script.

A cold winter weekend offered an ideal opportunity to curl up on the couch with a cozy blanket, a remote control and a stack of newly released movies. The films I chose were enjoyable and entertaining, but afterwards I found myself thinking—not about their storylines, heroes or villains—but about their predictability.

In the romantic comedy, after some absurd and amusing antics and near misses, the girl finally saw that Mr. Right had been right there all along. The drama also neatly resolved its characters' issues and challenges in 157 minutes. The hardened criminal discovered compassion, took responsibility for his actions and turned in his ill gotten gains, then returned to jail to enlighten and inspire other inmates to do likewise.

While we can learn a lot from movie characters' experiences and discoveries, it's useful to notice the impressions these productions make on our thinking, values and expectations. Considering how Cinderella's story has impacted generations of women's expectations of men, how are movie characters' goals, values and beliefs influencing our own? Are our expressed desires truly the yearnings of our own hearts, or are they merely concepts adopted from the silver screen? How can we tell?

After watching countless lives unfold on the big screen, many of us find that when real life shows up, loose threads and all, it feels like something's wrong. It's not supposed to be this way. Dad was not supposed to die before we had a chance to tell him how much we loved him. Our romantic hero is not supposed to marry someone else, much less stay happily married for a lifetime. Killers should not get away with murder—and yet they do. This discrepancy between real life and life as portrayed by movies can create serious cognitive dissonance for those of us who are unaware of this pervasive influence.

In Philadelphia in 2003, I introduced a new exercise into my Authentic Personal Branding workshops which required participants to describe their "dream lives." They were asked: If you had a magic wand and could recreate your life without time, physical, geographic or financial limitations, what would it be like? While most participants were able to generate lists of socially acceptable desires (a luxury home, a sports car, a million dollar jackpot, to be thin, to travel around the world, to be successful in business, etc.) no one could explain *why* they wanted these things or *what having them would do for them.* A few even complained the exercise was "too hard." They were right.

Bringing our heart's desires to the surface isn't easy, but it is important. For while fiction can inspire original thinking, allowing mainstream cultural ideals to masquerade as our authentic desires can cost us our very lives. We can't get back the years of effort and sacrifice we invested in getting what we thought we wanted.

To create exciting, fulfilling lives, we must first examine our soul-felt yearnings and distinguish them from the pre-packaged cultural ideals we buy into. (Do you really want to find your soul mate–or are you happy on your own? Will you truly be happier if you're 20 pounds lighter, or have perfect teeth?)

We need to develop the ability to tune out the razzle-dazzle clamoring of our culture and tune in to the gentle murmurings of our hearts. Now I won't pretend this is easy, for we are as enmeshed in our culture as peanuts are in the caramel of a Snickers bar. But by identifying our true desires, we can create lives that are incredibly personally rewarding. And when we truly believe we can have what we want, we get to watch in wonder as synchronicities unfold, creating outcomes that far exceed our original expectations.

So enjoy movies for their ability to present new ideas and information, but don't confuse their reality with your own. You can choose to live life as an independent producer, writing your original screenplay and starring in the lead role, or you can spend your life replaying the same roles over and over again.

Tips for writing, directing and starring in your own life-long feature film

✪ Look back to find times in your life when you were on top of the world, supremely happy and fulfilled. Write down as many as you can recall as stories (a minimum of three). Compare them to uncover common themes, consistent plot lines and similarities between the other characters who were involved. What sorts of activities and people do you consistently enjoy? What sorts of challenges bring out your best, time and time again? Who and what brings you down, makes you angry, wastes your time? This exercise will help you differentiate fantasies from authentic, achievable dreams.

❂ Make a list of everything you have declared you want and feel is important to you. Prioritize the list. Now explore your heart's desires by inviting your heart to expose its deepest yearnings. (You can do this by meditating, actively or passively, or by simply jotting down what comes up in your notebook or journal. Be sure to stock up on soap crayons if you get your best ideas in the shower!) Compile your notes into a new list that's ordered from what's most important to what's least important.

❂ Take a trip into the future, to the end of your life. What do you want to be able to say you have achieved? What do you want to be remembered for? How do you absolutely <u>not</u> want to be remembered?

Combine all of your outcomes to create a strong plot outline–then cast your co-stars, choose your location, sets, props and costumes, write your daily scenes to match your heart's desires and live the role of your life!

The Power of Two Words: New Woman

By Sherry J. Davis

Once your goal is established and you've set a plan, a strategy and a map of how to attain and achieve it, then life is about moving vigorously in that direction. During the journey you will slip up, make mistakes or have lazy days, rationalize to avoid a challenging situation and perhaps even veer off course. What's critical is how you handle these setbacks and detours to keep from getting stuck.

Most of us are very hard on ourselves at those times. It's important to remember we are human beings—humans being the best we can be. To forgive yourself quickly and move on toward your goal is a great gift you can give yourself. Go ahead and be mad, frustrated and disappointed with yourself if you need to, but then jump up, dust yourself off and say with conviction (silently if you must): **"New Woman."** You can say whatever feels right to you: "New Woman" or "New Person" or "New Me."

However you say it, forgive yourself, love yourself and get on with what is at hand.

People sometimes use one bump in the road or some failure as an excuse not to move on. It can be a justification that part of you was right after all to doubt your goal, that it won't, can't or isn't supposed to happen. A good and wise friend once told me that it's always best to admit your mistakes quickly, apologize if necessary and move on. Do it before anyone can even get upset about it. It's best to get these things over quickly. I agree. From my experience, mistakes just don't go away, and the longer they persist the worse they usually get. Like a sliver under your skin, if left alone it festers and becomes infected.

Declaring "New Woman" is a wonderful way to face our humanness and move forward. Try it, and I guarantee it will make life much easier, freer and happier for you.

Seven Keys To Rut-Free Living on the Road of Life

By Rhonda Hull

Are you stuck, stuck, stuck in a rut on the road of life? It's frustrating. Like a car stuck in a rut, you just spin your tires, rocking back and forth in place but never covering any ground. You know you should move forward, but instead of taking that small initial step, you perpetuate your "stuck-ness" by doing anything—and everything—else. You water the plants, pour another cup of coffee, check the mail, rearrange the papers on your desk, or call a friend. Yet what you resist persists, emptying you of energy, joy and enthusiasm.

So how do you get back on track, refill your gas tank and start moving again in the direction of your hopes and dreams? Here are seven keys to help you break free from your rut and go merrily on your way.

1. You gotta wanna

You have to step out of believing you're a victim of the school of hard knocks. You always have choices. Even though you can't always control the circumstances of your life, you *can* control the way you view them and the way you respond to them. Even though you may not have the fastest or newest car, you *can* decide what direction you're going to steer toward. Use the power of positive thinking to gain a fresh perspective and try a new path. Going down the same old road of thought patterns will not get you where you want to go if it's the *wrong* road, no matter how fast you drive.

2. Admit you're stuck

Once you're stuck, it's impossible to free yourself from your well-worn rut without first admitting to yourself that you're stuck. As odd as it sounds, even though you don't like being stuck, it can feel more familiar to you than facing the unknowns that come hand-in-hand with change. Acknowledging that you're stuck is essential for getting back on the road to freedom with a renewed sense of energy and purpose.

3. Discover what it is you want

You may feel totally detoured from knowing your own dreams. All of your energy may have gone into fulfilling everyone else's needs. But your dreams and longings are equally as important. Remember, you teach people how to treat you by how you treat yourself. The journey of self-love is the tow rope that pulls you free. Dare to declare the things you want and involve yourself with the people and things that feed your inner spirit. Discern when you respond with an authentic "yes," or when you say "yes" out of obligation. A truthful "no" is truly more loving than a resentful "yes," and affords you the energy you need to move forward out of your rut. Leaps of faith are great, but small steps are okay, too. Set realistic expectations so you can experience a sense of success rather than setting yourself up for failure.

4. Shine light on your excuses

You've got them. We all do. You're too tired. It's too late. You don't have enough energy. There's not enough time. You don't have enough money. Everyone else needs your attention. Work is too demanding. By dragging your excuses out into the open, you become more conscious. Consciousness leads to greater creativity and energy. With energy you become proactive. With action and a sense of your own worth comes freedom from your stuck place.

5. Vision

Your thoughts influence your reality. Stretch to imagine being rut-free. Visualize yourself full of energy, direction, passion and clarity. Allow the feeling to penetrate your body and your Spirit as if what you dream of is already so. Believing is seeing, even though you were taught the opposite. By seeing it and feeling it as if it is already so, you begin to move forward on your journey, taking the necessary and incremental steps toward embracing change.

6. See mistakes as an opportunity to learn

Make a list of ideas. Complete your list before passing judgment and consider every possibility—no matter how big, small, crazy or impossible it may seem. Allow mistakes to become your opportunity to learn. If Edison hadn't made a few mistakes, you'd still be reading this in the dark!

7. Just start moving

Yoda, from *Star Wars*, reminds us to "Do or do not, there is no try." Trying is a state of inaction. Even the smallest step is important. The size doesn't matter; what matters is that you dare to take the step. It informs the Universe that you are ready to fly. If you're not sure what to do, just do anything other than what you're doing in your rut. Find a mentor, take a class, ask for help, read a book, and most important, learn to trust that your inner knowing will guide you. Apply everything you learn from your mistakes. Reach for excellence rather than perfection, and remember that life is a journey, not a destination. Savor every moment.

These seven keys offer you a nudge to access the flow and help you to move out of your rut to make life meaningful. Your commitment to making your words and actions match empowers you to make the most out of this present moment, this precious present. For after all, life is precious and it is a present…a gift amidst a magical mystery.

Now is the only moment there truly is, and what you do with each moment to infuse it with love is what creates a journey of contentment, regardless of the circumstances. Will you choose to stay in your rut of blame and self-doubt, or will you access your courage and creativity, so life can be a joy ride every step of the way?

Take A Minute To Breathe

By Ava Evans

People often get stuck in stressful situations or anxiety, sometimes many times during a day, so this is a quick time out. If you can just relax your body and calm your mind, sometimes that's all you need to relax, focus and move on.

This technique is used to reduce your stress or anxiety levels and is helpful in conjunction with hypnosis in smoking cessation and weight control; it's easy to do and will almost immediately relax you. This breathing exercise—which only takes one to two minutes—can change your feelings from tension and stress to a calmer state.

I am a Certified Hypnotherapist and this is one of the techniques I teach my clients so they can feel more in control of their lives.

Begin by sitting at the edge of a chair, sofa or bed, making sure you have enough room to stretch your arms. With your eyes closed, take a slow, deep breath inflating your stomach like a balloon, slowly bringing your breath up into your chest. At the same time, extend your arms down the sides of your legs, then slowly raise them, ending with your palms together above your head. Hold your breath and that position for a second or two. Begin releasing your breath and slowly deflating your stomach while moving your arms down to where you began. You can do this in sets of four, two to four times a day or as needed. While doing this exercise you are oxygenating your body and calming your mind.

If it's inconvenient to use your arms, on each slow, deep inhale, put the index finger and thumb of each hand together. Now pick a calming word to use as you exhale, repeating the word silently and relaxing your fingers. Repeat until you feel yourself changing your emotional state.

The more you use these techniques the better they work; it's like a muscle that gets stronger the more it is used. Breathe, relax and enjoy!

When All Else Fails, Try Something Unconventional

By Lynda Malerstein

You've read all the self-help books. You say your affirmations daily. You have a terrific business plan. Your enthusiastic support system says "You go, girl!"

Still, you feel like there's a bowling ball in your stomach when you sit down in front of your "to do" list. A team of butterflies plays the Super Bowl inside you when you think about speaking in front of that group of colleagues. In spite of your positive thoughts and actions, those old negative messages keep popping up again and again.

There's a powerful and very simple technique you can use to help break through those uncomfortable feelings. It's called Emotional Freedom Techniques (EFT). It started out as a New Age kind of therapy but now is being used by professional people all over the world.

By tapping on certain points on your body while focusing on the negative emotions you wish to release, you can quickly and easily reduce and even eliminate fears, anxieties, cravings and blocks to creative performance.

The tapping points are taken from the Chinese Medicine model, in which there are pathways of energy that run through your body. When the energy is blocked and inhibited from flowing freely through those pathways, you can experience mental discomfort and even physical pain. According to Gary Craig, the founder of EFT, "The cause of all negative emotions is a disruption in the body's energy system."

By tapping on a series of acupressure points, EFT helps you balance your body's energy system and restore positive flow. Once you learn it, you can use it over and over on issues of all kinds. It's a powerful tool, and you carry your toolbox with you at all times on the ends of your fingers.

You begin by acknowledging the negative thought or feeling in a set-up phrase: "Even though I have this ***fear*** (the negative emotion), I deeply and completely accept myself." Other examples might be: "Even though I am ***angry*** at Joe for …." or "Even though I am ***disappointed*** in myself for letting John reject my idea without a fight….". As you focus on that negative thought, you tap using two fingers of one hand on the side of the other hand under the little finger. It's called the karate chop point, because if you were going to break a board in karate, this is where your hand would meet the wood. Five to seven taps is about right for each of these steps. Do the set-up phrase three times, tapping on the karate chop point as you repeat it.

Next, you just focus on the negative emotion by itself using a reminder phrase: "this ***fear***" (or "this ***anger***" or "this ***disappointment***;" whatever the emotion is). You don't need to say the whole sentence again since your subconscious mind absorbed it in the set-up phrase. Tap—again using any two fingers—on the area between your eyebrows just above the bridge of the nose, repeating "***this …***".

Continue repeating and focusing on the reminder phrase "***this …***" as you tap on these additional areas: the side of the corner of your eye, just under your eye at the top of your cheekbone, under your nose, under your chin in the hollow place, about one inch under either collar bone, and under your arm about where the band of your bra would be. At each point you tap with two fingers about five to seven times. It doesn't matter which side of the body you tap. When you have finished the round, take a deep breath through your nose and exhale fully through your mouth.

You might expand the set-up phrase to be something like: "Even though I have ***this fear*** that if I call this banker, he'll laugh at me because I believe my idea isn't very marketable, I still deeply and completely accept myself." The reminder phrase will then be "***this fear and belief***." Once you have tapped down the level of anxiety, you can then tap in your affirmation: "And I choose to believe that my idea is sound, and if this banker turns me down, I will find someone else who is more visionary." This is just a simple example.

You can notice dramatic results if you test it on a mild headache. You start with, "Even though I have this ***headache***, I deeply and completely accept myself," tapping on the karate chop point. Tap "***this headache***" between the eyebrows, under the eye, to the side of one eye, under one eye, under the nose, under the chin, under the collar bone and under the arm. Take a deep breath and exhale and notice the relief.

I have used EFT to help clients overcome sales-call resistance, fear of public speaking, insomnia, general anxiety and sugar cravings. I have helped them with sports performance, writer's block, self-confidence—the list could go on and on.

What I have shared above is a very basic and simplified introduction to EFT. To find out more, go to the EFT website at www.emofree.com. There you can download a free 80-page manual and read hundreds of success stories from people from all walks of life.

Here's to tapping in to your success.

Maybe You Just Need A Good Shaking Up!

By Nita Vallens, Psy.D.

In order to break through barriers, it can sometimes help to shake your life up a little—or a lot! Simply by taking the time to treat yourself a little better, it's possible to climb out of a rut. Or consider approaching ordinary tasks differently to inspire a change in your thinking. But my best advice is don't do it alone.

Do something everyday to honor yourself. This means be intentionally selfish–put yourself first, and then you'll be in better shape to help others. Some ideas are:

- ✪ Enjoy a bubble bath with candles
- ✪ Eat something healthy you cooked yourself
- ✪ Take a walk in an inspiring area
- ✪ Go to a park and push off on a swing
- ✪ Save time to journal at the end of the day, or perhaps start a specific gratitude journal
- ✪ Read old journals to appreciate your progress
- ✪ Sleep in or take a nap
- ✪ Change your pace–slow it down or speed it up

Do something different everyday. This gets you thinking outside the box and reprograms your neural network. Some examples are:

- ✪ Take a different route to work

❂ Move some furniture around
❂ Learn a new software program
❂ Borrow a friend's dog and take him for a walk
❂ Listen to a kind of music you don't usually seek out, especially from a culture that uses a completely different musical scale
❂ Shop in a different store, or try a farmers market
❂ Turn off the TV and read instead
❂ Visit some edgy art galleries
❂ Hang out with someone much older or younger and find out what they're thinking about
❂ Try a new cuisine—Ethiopian anyone?
❂ Read a publication you don't usually read
❂ Think back to your childhood and do something fun that you miss, like riding a bike or skating

Do get daily support.

This is the most important element. Great things do not happen in a vacuum. Try the buddy system: arrange to speak to a friend for just a few minutes every morning and set between one and three simple goals each. Committing to another person and revving each other up is a great way to begin the day. Make the call no more than five minutes long—you can talk later about other things, but keep to the structure and it will build momentum for you.

Stuck? Take A Hike!

By Dina Weinberg

Solvitur ambulando. It is solved by walking.
~ Saint Augustine

It's common to all executives today—running fast, so fast that it's a challenge to truly focus and forecast the future. With Blackberries, cell phones, e-mail, PDAs, laptops and pagers, it can be difficult to make an excuse to be out of touch. It has become the norm rather than a choice to be always available. So how do you create time to simply think?

Most people have heard of Outward Bound, the 60-year-old company that provides experiential programs for young people to build character, leadership abilities and self-esteem. According to Outward Bound literature, through challenge and adventure you walk away with a renewed sense of "team work, self-knowledge, tenacity, self-reliance, leadership and the ability to go beyond self-imposed limitations."

If it works for kids, why not for adults? In fact, why not for business owners, entrepreneurs, executives and leaders? Many organizations have an annual getaway where teams go offsite to another location and participate in team building programs to inspire motivation, communication and collaboration. But what happens when you are not at an offsite event? The phone is still ringing, you are still receiving hundreds of emails, and the Blackberry doesn't quit. You need to create your own getaway for yourself and even your team.

Many of my clients find being outdoors is a remedy. Some even comment that simply being active, getting outside and out of their own head space does provide time to think and check in with themselves. Even Plato extolled the virtues of having an outdoor experience: "The moral value of exercises and sports far outweigh the physical value."

As leaders, to break the cycle and gain new perspectives, to reach fresh solutions, being outdoors away from the distractions of your typical office environment is critical. Take a walk, hit some balls on the golf course, or simply go for a run, then follow that up with some focused self-examination. The bottom line is: you must have a purpose and an end result in mind.

Here are some clear benefits of getting outside:

❂ Creates focus, inspires motivation and induces problem solving and clarity

❂ Gets you out of the office, out of your head and out of linear thinking

❂ Inspires collaboration and solutions outside of the typical office environment

As a result of my busy clients needing a break, we sometimes hold our sessions outdoors and take to the hills, go hiking and devise new and creative solutions to complex problems. We break them down into simple, manageable steps and inevitably, each person walks away with a gem of a new idea.

But you can simulate the brainstorming and collaboration by yourself, outside of costly team-building activities.

Getting started is simple:

1. Pick an issue or subject needing clarity. Is it succession planning? Are you looking to timeline a new project? Forecast your career development beyond being a CEO?

2. Ask yourself a question that will move you forward, such as: What do I want? Why do I want it? What meaning will it bring? What are my challenges? What are my opportunities? What do I need to focus on? What are the resources at my fingertips to get it done?

3. Limit yourself to one major question (otherwise you might find yourself out all day and all night!).

4. Select a location. Is it the golf course? Beach? Hiking trail? Pick a place with a vista—it will help you to imagine, dream and get past your notion of what the solution needs to look like.

5. Before you venture out, set an intention and allow yourself to come up with outrageous ideas.

6. Bring a pad and pen to record your thoughts and new ideas.

7. Write down one question at the top of the page (one page per question).

8. When you get to your destination use the following formula:

✪ Exercise for ten minutes—hike, walk on the beach, hit those golf balls

❂ Stop and write for ten minutes—anything that answers the question at the top of the page. Don't edit. Even if you write "I have no idea what I'm writing about." Begin to get any internal chatter out.

❂ Be active again for another ten minutes

❂ Stop and brainstorm on solutions, ten minutes

❂ Activity again, ten minutes

❂ Final brainstorm, ten minutes

❂ Repeat the process for each question

You can make these stretches of time longer or shorter, it's up to you. However you do it, this process will get you out of your day-to-day thinking and move you out of your own way. Recently, I had a client, a senior level executive, who was brainstorming on his team development. He went to the batting cage, did the writing exercises and came back with unique solutions that he admitted were never originally on his radar.

So when you want new paradigms and resolution to any issues, look to the outdoors as a resource to further your visions. When you stand at the mountain top and look at the vista, how can you possibly set limitations? The sky is indeed the limit.

Feng Shui: Intention In Physical Form

By Sandi Rose Miller

Feng Shui is often regarded as a magic bullet, that once everything in your environment is positioned properly, makes your life work like a charm. Your stuck c*hi* (chi is just another word for energy) begins flowing harmoniously, and bad luck turns to good, creating synchronistic benevolence all over the place.

Truth is, many times my clients *do* experience amazingly rapid shifts, virtually out of the blue, by applying simple Feng Shui basics. However, it's my experience that Feng Shui is *not* a magic bullet, and the clients who free up their chi, become unstuck and create lasting benefits, are those who really understand the true power *behind* any Feng Shui "cure."

Let's face it, if all it took to create an abundant life was to have your front door face the best direction, your couch placed in the power position and for the right Feng Shui enhancements to be placed in the correct locations—then I believe we'd all have taken those steps a long time ago, and our lives would already be magnificent.

Contrary to some schools of thought, it has been my experience that Feng Shui doesn't directly affect the space you live or work in. Rather, Feng Shui directly affects your mental, physical and spiritual *connection and response* to your space.

For example, let's say you're interested in bringing more abundance into your life in any area:

health, wealth, relationship, career, etc. Your first step toward upgrading your environmental chi is to choose an object you particularly like; in Feng Shui these objects are called chi-enhancements. Let's say you fall in love with a beautiful, big-leafed plant and see it as representative of the financial abundance you'd like to attract. Choose a plant you really like with large, lush leaves and one that feels welcoming—spiky leaves give the message: stay away.

You then place your new plant in an area of your home or office where you will see it daily and often. The new plant *anchors* your *intention* in physical form and acts as a reminder of your desire to increase your flow of financial abundance and your willingness to do whatever it takes today to get it. I like to think of Feng Shui as intention in physical form.

Very shortly, you might notice a definite increase in your bank account. Do you believe (as taught in some forms of Feng Shui) that you happened to choose the *perfect* money-attracting plant, and its magic is now working in your favor? Or do you think maybe you lucked into placing your plant in your home's *ideal* money-attracting location (as also taught in some Feng Shui methods)?

In my experience, the true power of attracting wealth in any area has much less to do with the actual chi-enhancer and its placement, than it does with your increased focus and intention directed toward your desire. Your intention is immensely powerful, and the more you focus it like a laser in the direction of your goals, the faster they manifest in your reality.

I've found when you shift the energy in your environment (enhance with Feng Shui and place your intention in physical form), you then shift the energy in your mind (create positive beliefs and feelings that you are worthy, fortunate and open to receive), which changes the actions you take toward manifesting your dreams. As Winston Churchill said, "First we shape our houses, then our houses shape us."

The true power of real Feng Shui energy shifts—as with any lasting change—comes from within. In all honesty, you can do outer or environmental Feng Shui until the cows come home, but if underneath it all, your life is being run by negative or limiting thoughts and beliefs, no amount of outer Feng Shui cures will make a difference. We must feel abundant to manifest true, lasting wealth.

Feng Shui is an excellent tool for creating environments that support our hopes and dreams. One evening at a book signing, a gentleman asked, "If Feng Shui success is dependant primarily upon doing steadfast mental monitoring and choosing which beliefs we allow to run us, why bother doing any environmental/outer Feng Shui?" Excellent question! The reason we need a physical reminder system is because we're human. We live in a physical world that is moving incredibly fast, and we forget what we said we were going to do to reach our goals last week…or even just yesterday! Feng Shui anchors our desires and intentions in physical form, and combined with healthy, positive inner/chi, attracts our desires from the Universe like a giant magnet.

Feng Shui manifestation process quick guide

❂ Get clear about your dreams, goals and intentions.

❂ Choose an object/chi-enhancer you love that represents the desired result of your focus in the previous step (i.e., abundance, vibrant health, loving relationships, rewarding career).

❂ Place your object/chi-enhancer in a highly visible location where you will see it regularly.

❂ Remind yourself whenever you see your special object/chi-enhancer exactly what it is you most intend to attract into your life, and take any action you can take *right now* to move you closer to your goal.

❂ Celebrate ALL wins…large or little!

Clarity Is A High Octane Fuel

By Oriana Green

Sometimes what keeps us stuck is just confusion. Do you feel like your brain is overstuffed with information, deadlines, unfinished projects, To Do lists and schedules ad infinitum? Worse yet, do you know or sense you have wonderful new ideas lurking in there, just waiting to be uncovered and developed? Or perhaps you're trying to make one important decision—whether to take a job offer or whether to end a relationship.

Overwhelm happens to us all. The solution is clarity. When you get clear about what matters to you most, things that are time wasters almost magically disappear from your life, because you *know* what you need to be doing at any given moment. (And that could be relaxing and refreshing your busy brain!)

Few of us are so finely scheduled that there aren't pockets of time during each day which we fritter away mindlessly. And that's part of getting clear—becoming more mindful about how you spend your time. Time is the most valuable commodity you have—you can always make more money, but you can't make more time. It's the one truly level playing field in life; we all get the same 24 hours every day to manage as we please. So how well do you use yours?

I promise you that if you get clear on your priorities, the time to deal with what's important will be there. So how do you gain this elusive clarity? One way is by making lists. Start with a list of qualities and aspects of your work life that you enjoy and dislike. For instance, on the first list might be: love interacting with people face to face, like traveling around the country meeting new people, enjoy seeing the results of my work in meetings. On the second list might be: resist handling details, hate spending too much time at the computer, detest number crunching.

Then do the same thing with regard to your personal lifestyle. This list might include: I need my weekends to be sacrosanct, or I only want to work four days a week, or I don't mind bringing work home in the evenings. Think about vacation time, being able to attend your child's school play, whether you're a morning person or not, how much of a break you need to recharge at lunch time. These are all quality of life factors that often don't get enough attention when you evaluate a particular job. In the interest of keeping the wolf from the door, some women don't believe they can afford to worry about those things, but that's a real mistake.

Now make a list of all projects that you've already started and a separate list of ideas you think you'd like to pursue. Then review these lists through the filter of your newly clarified values to see which things are in alignment with what really matters most to you. You could even rank the items on your list if there are a lot of them. The ones that have no underpinning of synchronization with what you value are ones to release. You will never feel the fire and passion to see them through to completion, or if you somehow flog yourself to do it anyway, the result will by unsatisfying.

Returning to the above list of likes and dislikes, would someone with that list ever feel happy overseeing the company website or taking charge of budgeting a big program? No way. This is a classic people person who needs to be out interacting with co-workers and clients every day. She would feel stuck and frustrated in an office facing a computer screen all day. This is an extreme example, so you will probably have to work a little harder to notice how your lists mesh—or don't.

Examine your project lists for the things that have the highest resonance with your values and with your style of working and living. Those are the ones that will be easiest to develop and the ones that will give you the most joy and satisfaction. Or that's the job you should be looking for. Or the life partner. It doesn't matter what the specifics are, just condensing these things into lists, then filtering them through each other, can help you solve any dilemma.

Once you are clear about what you want, the process to get there becomes merely a question of mechanics. And the energy that is freed up once you release uncertainty and confusion is astonishing.

Loss Is A Fact of Life, and the Velocity and Intensity of Loss Increases with Age

By Jan Blakeley Holman

Some of us accept that truth and some of us struggle with it. I am a struggler. Loss immobilizes me, and for the past decade I have experienced a lot of loss. During that time, two of my closest friends died, my marriage ended, I've had a few failed love relationships, one of my dogs died of old age, another after being hit by a car, and my relationship with a long-term employer ended.

Although I've had a sense for quite awhile that I wasn't good at accepting loss, it's taken me a long time to figure out how to regroup and move forward once I've experienced one. Finally, I think I get it.

To figure out what would help me regain momentum after a loss, I took myself through a process where I first identified those elements of life that bring me joy, give me hope and move me forward. Then I made a conscious effort to make sure those things are an ongoing part of my life.

Here are my motivators:

❂ **People.** One of the common themes we heard the victims of Hurricane Katrina say was, "I can lose my house and all of my possessions, but I need my people to survive." Appreciate the people in your life: your family, friends and co-workers. If you don't have any, find some. Or if you don't feel like you have enough people in your life, get some more. When you put yourself in situations where you interact and bond with others, you open yourself up to opportunities that change your life and move you forward.

Losing a job can be unsettling for a variety of reasons. First, there's the obvious concern of financial loss. Second, there's the truth for many of us that work defines who we are and gives us a sense of purpose. Finally, when we leave an employer, we upset important long-term business relationships.

Like many others, I experienced a huge sense of loss when my job was eliminated at the company where I spent the majority of my career. When I left the company, I had trouble getting my bearings. Still in mourning two years later, I jumped at the chance to return to my former employer. When that job was eliminated a year and a half later, I'd had enough! It took two job losses and a ton of frustration for me to finally figure out that it wasn't the company I missed—it was the people.

Believing I wasn't the only one who'd left the company and missed her former colleagues, I decided to create an ex-employee network for myself and my former colleagues. I began with a list of e-mail addresses and telephone numbers for 50 other people who'd also left the company voluntarily or because their jobs were eliminated. I picked a date, booked a room for an event and asked another former colleague to design an invitation to the networking event. The connections were made. While the network is still in its infancy, the list has grown to over 300 people, and we've had three well attended ex-employee events. It's given us an opportunity to reconnect with colleagues and rekindle former friendships.

❂ **Nature.** I remember the first time I recognized feeling joy. It was during a conference I was attending at a resort in Arizona. Very early one morning I decided to get some exercise by taking a walk. It was daybreak. No one else was up. Nature was my only companion—the sound of birds, the feel of crispiness in the air and the smell of grass and trees. I was overwhelmed by the feelings of joy and optimism. Ever since that experience, I've understood the healing power of nature and have taken advantage of opportunities to pay attention to my surroundings, get outside and experience nature.

❂ **Pets.** Some of us are animal lovers, some of us aren't. With three dogs, I count myself among the former. Understanding how important my dogs are to me and knowing they live relatively short lives, I make a point of connecting with them every day. I include them in my daily routine, I talk to them and I watch them play. They return my attention with responsiveness and love that inspires me and gives me the energy to face each day.

❂ **Passion.** We all have passions. Mine is photography. I find that I lose myself when I take photographs. I have no sense of time. But more important, I have no sense of inertia. When I'm taking photographs, I see possibilities and look for opportunities to take more pictures. For me creativity is a great energizer and motivator.

❂ **Routine.** One solution to not moving forward is to just get moving. The great thing about doing chores is they don't typically require a lot of concentration. Most of us use chores as an opportunity to let our minds wander. When your mind wanders, you can forget about your troubles and open the door to creativity. Creativity spawns possibilities, and possibilities create energy that gets us going. Some of my most creative ideas have taken shape while I was sweeping the floor or mowing the lawn.

If you want to get yourself moving again, take some time to figure out what is really important to you. Once you know what motivates you, make a point of incorporating those things into your life. I've learned to regain momentum after a loss by connecting with people, experiencing nature, loving my pets, embracing my passions and throwing myself into my routine.

Quick Tips for Getting Unstuck

By Laura Handke Jones

Are you feeling stuck about money? Don't seem to be bringing in the prosperity and abundance you know you deserve? Then try what I did, and form a group of women, using Barbara Stanny's *Secrets of Six Figure Women* as the initial impetus and required reading. Simply having the insight, wisdom, generosity and support of like-minded women makes a huge difference. It's not really about money. It's about our understanding of money and feelings of self-worth.

❂ Do you feel stuck about your purpose? Then sit down and write a letter to yourself. Make it a message about how you are living your life, as if everything you want is already there in your life right now. Let your imagination run wild, and please don't limit yourself in any way, shape or form. Truly allow your spirit to come through. For added impact, you could make copies of the letter, prepare them for mailing and have a friend send one to you every few months to remind you of your vision.

❂ Are you feeling stuck about where to go after writing your total imaginative message to yourself? Form a circle with like-minded women, and allow yourself to dream even bigger, go beyond the imaginable and help each other with perceived obstacles.

❂ Still stuck after all this? It might be because you're not vibrating at the same energetic level as that which you wish to attract. Consider checking out *Excuse Me, Your Life is Waiting*, written by the late Lynn Grabhorn. Give yourself a positive pep talk every day for around 10 minutes, and don't just speak it aloud, feel it in your body. For example: "It's so AWESOME to be completely debt-free; I can't even remember what it felt like to have so much credit card debt! It's so WONDERFUL to have only a few bills every month and to pay them quickly! I'm so HAPPY to have a growing investment portfolio and know I never need to work again. Yet I LOVE working so much, because I know how I am touching people. My home environment is peaceful, nurturing and joyous. I LOVE being in my home! Everyone I touch is helped by my work and I'm GRATEFUL knowing this."

Ritual To Unlock Blocks

By Barbara Biziou

This is one of my favorite things to do when I feel stuck. I use it often with clients and they love it. It is very empowering to physically release stuck energy. It seems to free the mind from the task of performing and, instead, opens it to expressing.

Version one

❂ **Intention:** to free your creative energy.

❂ **Ingredients:** piece of cardboard and dark-colored markers, cookie tray, water, hammer, orange candle, essential oils.

You can begin this two-part process by writing your goals on a piece of cardboard. Put it in a tray of water and place it in your freezer. When the water has turned to ice, begin the second part of the ritual by lighting a candle and spraying or diffusing the essence you've chosen. After inhaling deeply, exhale slowly as you hold the cold tray, imagining all of your creativity trapped in the block of ice. Take several quick, shallow breaths as you concentrate on the feeling of constriction. Are you holding it in your neck? In your shoulders? Can you feel it in your stomach?

Turn the tray upside down on the floor and tap the bottom until the ice falls out. Cover it with a dishtowel, protect yourself and, with all your might, smash the ice with the hammer. As you crack the physical ice that contains your piece of cardboard, you're breaking whatever is blocking you.

Sit quietly and feel the space you've created. Imagine accomplishing everything you desire.

Anoint the candle with a few drops of the essential oil. Light the candle as a reminder of the power of your creative spirit. Ground this ritual by taking one action to move you closer to your dreams.

Version two

❂ **Intention:** to release negative thoughts and emotions as well as dysfunctional patterns.

❂ **Ingredients:** inexpensive plate, permanent marker, hammer, garbage bag, essence of grapefruit, lemon or orange.

I find that expressing aloud my fears and the things that keep me stuck is the first step in moving forward. Begin by sitting quietly with the plate in your lap. Take a few deep breaths and allow yourself to become aware of all the voices in your head that stop you from moving forward. Be conscious of the fear, anger, resentment, disappointment and other feelings that may surface. As the voices talk, write them on the plate. *It's too hard* or *You're not good enough*, *You missed your chance*, *Why bother* or *It's too scary*. Ask for help in recognizing the negative emotions and habits that steal your energy. It may help to imagine you are talking to a wise elder, a favorite teacher or a spiritual advisor.

Some of the themes that seem to come up in every group ritual I have facilitated are: fear of failure, needing outside approval, unworthiness and perfectionism.

When you are finished, breathe deeply for a minute or two and then read aloud what you have written. You can speak to your pet, your reflection in a mirror or to a plant. Your audience does not matter, but speaking aloud does, because it brings the words—symbolically and literally—into the open. At the end say, "I am now ready to gently and easily release everything on this plate."

Wrap the plate in a heavy-duty trash bag. Place it on the floor, on a cutting board, outside on the patio or anywhere you can smash it safely. Now take the hammer and break the plate. Throw out the bag, knowing you are opening space in your life for new people, projects and support.

Experience your new space and place a few drops of essence of orange, grapefruit or lemon (use only pure essential oils) in a diffuser, or cut up fresh lemon, orange or grapefruit and inhale the aroma.

Don't Get Stuck with Empty Pockets

By Marcia Brixey

Are your dreams on hold for lack of funds? Women who attend my Money Wi$e Women Forums often tell me they don't have any extra money to save or invest. I don't believe them. Why? Because I used to say the same thing. Awareness is half the battle. I advise women to take the Money Wi$e Women 14-Day Challenge, which is simply writing down everything you buy for at least 14 days.

Try not to spend any differently—just write it all down. Take a small notebook or a blank checkbook register and write down everything you buy with cash, your ATM card, debit card, credit card, check, etc. I've yet to meet someone who didn't find something they could cut back on. Usually it's the incidentals that do us in. Things like lattes, bottled water, snacks, newspapers, magazines, books, eating out, etc. How many times have you gone to the ATM, withdrawn $60 and two days later wondered where it all went?

Tracking your spending will also heighten your awareness of your buying patterns and make you think about the money you spend. For example, the next time you're in the grocery store checkout line and pick up a magazine, I hope you'll look at the price and consider: Do I really want to spend $5.95 on this magazine? Whether or not you choose to buy the magazine is your decision. It's not about deprivation. It's about *awareness* and making conscious, informed choices.

Tracking your spending is the first step in creating a spending plan. Did you notice I used the words *spending plan* instead of *budget*? The word budget reminds me of the word diet—and makes me think of shortage, self-denial and regret. Budget makes me think of things I want but can't afford. A spending plan puts *you* in control. It allows you to determine what's important to purchase and what you can buy just because it's there. A spending plan is a roadmap for your trip to becoming debt-free or having savings for emergencies or future opportunities.

I love to shop, but I seldom end up taking everything in my basket home with me. My friends give me a hard time, because when we're shopping together, I review all of the items in my basket when I get to the sales counter. I look at each item and ask myself five questions, which I call the **Checkout Checklist:**

- Do I really want this?
- Do I need this?
- Will I use this?
- Am I buying this just because it's on sale?
- Do I really love this?

This is a great way to have fun shopping but not end up with everything in your basket. That being said, I'm not perfect, and sometimes I do end up with something that doesn't meet the Checkout Checklist test. But I keep my receipts and return a purchase if I decide I'm not going to use it.

A few more tips to trim your spending:

❂ Observe the 24-hour rule. Before you buy anything that costs more than $100, wait 24 hours. If you see something you really want and it costs more than $100, put it on hold. If you still want it the next day, go back and buy it. Most of the time, you'll forget what it was by the next day.

❂ Commit to not using your credit cards, checks or debit card for one week. Pay cash for everything. Try keeping a $100 bill in your wallet. It's much more difficult to spend a hundred dollar bill than it is to fork over five twenties or use a credit card. When shopping, ask yourself: Would I buy this item if I were paying cash? You'll probably discover it's much more difficult to spend cash than to use some form of paper or plastic.

❂ Before you buy something, think about how many hours you had to work to pay for it. For example, if you're buying an $80 dress and you earn $14.55 an hour (after taxes are withheld), you worked 5-1/2 hours for the dress. Is it really worth that much of your effort?

❂ Don't buy something just because it's on sale. Everyone loves a bargain, but if you're not going to use it, don't buy it. This has been a really hard habit for me to break. Every time I find something on sale that I think I want to buy, I stop and ask myself: Do I really need this, or am I buying it just because it's on sale? Most of the time I don't buy it. After-Christmas shopping is a really hard time for me. Wrapping paper and cards are always on sale dirt-cheap, and if I'm not careful I find myself in a buying frenzy. Once I get home and put my purchases away, I discover I have enough wrapping paper and cards for the next ten years. Does that sound familiar?

Be careful with gift buying. We tend to spend lots of money on gifts for others, especially during the holiday season. Review your gift list to determine if you really need to give presents to everyone on the list. Make a list of the people you plan to buy gifts for this year and stick to it! Why not make your gifts from the heart? They mean more, and isn't that what gift giving is all about?

Some heartfelt gift ideas:

❂ A gift certificate for a day of chores, yard work, house cleaning, window washing or car washing.

❂ A gift certificate to spend the day together doing something fun. Our parents and grandparents often appreciate the gift of time more than a store-bought gift. One Christmas my husband gave me a handmade card that read: Good for one day trip to the coast with Steve and our dogs, Scruffy and Missy.

❂ Cook a week's worth of dinners, freeze them and deliver to someone who's too busy or unable to cook.

❂ For children, purchase a U.S. Savings Bond, open a mutual fund or contribute to their future through an Education Savings Account. Both parents and grandparents can purchase any of the above.

❂ Offer to take a child to an art or science museum, and give mom a break in the bargain.

❂ Make handmade cards, including thank you, sympathy, get well, birthday, congratulations, etc. This is a good project for parents and children to do together for grandparents.

I think you can see that finding small ways to save money could add up to a big investment in your dreams.

Re-open Your Intuition by Shifting to A Different Part of Your Brain

By Penney Peirce

I usually feel blocked (and often exhausted) when I've been in my head too much, trying to solve problems using my "enterpriser mind" or "masculine mind"—that part of my awareness that can compartmentalize, analyze, formulate, catalyze and force. If I don't have an idea that excites me and makes me lean toward it, I notice I'm often trying to *make* things happen with will power, and inevitably there is a "should" involved somewhere under the surface. I might have gone too far along one course of exploration or action but think I "should" milk it to the very end or that I "should" be loyal, consistent, or diligently disciplined to show I'm a good person. The course isn't providing good results anymore, but I can't find my way to a new path.

I've learned over many years of working with intuition that the soul never says "should," but speaks instead of "I want, I enjoy, I'm appreciative of, I'm curious about. . ." In these dead-end-type situations, I have forgotten about pleasure and enthusiasm, which I now hold to be very high spiritual forces and a gauge for activities that flow from my favorite feeling: natural childlike motivation. My soul in its sanity won't let me go farther without joy and the involvement of all of me.

On the other hand, I might be trying to force a change, because I don't want to glean the last bits of the lesson I've been working on, the part that might force me to change my comfortable but unconscious habits were I to push on. For instance, I've often thought I needed to move to a new geographic area—and have spent countless hours seeking ways to get it to happen—when what I really needed was to love the place I was already living in and let it give more to me, and I to it. Easier to jump out of the fire than face some core truths that might emerge in stillness!

In those situations, I was totally blocked in my ability to move to another location. Nothing would line up. My soul wouldn't let me proceed in the direction I wanted, because what I really needed was to move deeper, not forward. Here, getting unstuck was tied to looking for the good reason I was immobilized and reframing it from being stuck to being fully present.

When I'm stuck, it often helps to shift to a different part of my brain. I teach that intuition, which I consider the voice of the soul or heart, appears in different ways depending on what level of the brain we're using. At the level of the reptile brain, guidance and intuition appear as "truth and anxiety signals"—subtle expansion and contraction of the body. We are attracted or repulsed, warm or cool, bubbly or dull. In the midbrain, intuition takes on the flavors and colors of our five senses. We might listen for the little voice, or feel for the right vibrations, or look for the flash or vision of what to do. In the upper neocortex, intuition looks like abstract, conceptual information, patterns, verbal definitions and meanings.

If you're stuck in your upper brain, struggling with meanings, fixed definitions and concepts, try dropping down to your midbrain and pay attention to simply sensing the world. Go outside—feel the sun, moon, wind; listen to the subtle sounds in the environment. Or move around to music, make a collage of magazine pictures that please you, taste a few foods thoroughly without verbal commentary, walk past some shops or the different rooms in your house and smell what wafts through the doors.

Take your attention off problem-solving or worrying (which is praying for what you don't want), and become more like an animal: unaware of time. Use your reptile brain to take you on a walk without an agenda. Turn left when your body wants to turn left, for no reason. Stop to look closely at, or merge into, an interesting flower or leaf. Find similarities between yourself and a beautifully designed garden or building or tree. Seeing similarities increases your intuition, which is direct knowing from your soul. Dropping into an experiential reality recharges and awakens your body, which is a powerful source of true motivation.

If you can open these intuitive pathways from the lower parts of the brain back to the upper brain, you'll soon find thoughts arising from the fresh, clean core of yourself—honest insights that suddenly shift the situation that was causing you to feel stuck. These insights present themselves quite matter-of-factly, right in front of your nose, and often as soon as you take the pressure off trying to solve the problem. For example: *Oh, I'm not supposed to move yet—I think I'll plant a new vegetable garden here instead.* Or *I'd rather get back into my watercolor painting for awhile, and not try to market my sales training courses.*

By shifting to the deeper, more primitive, animal-like parts of your brain, your soul can speak to you directly through your body. And interestingly, planting the garden or painting the watercolor—which seem totally unrelated to becoming more successful in your career—may be the vehicle that brings the next insight. You might consider integrating art into your sales training, or starting a learning center where you already live to bring more clients to you, instead of you going to them.

Keep Your Toolkit Packed

By Vickie Jenkins

As a media coach, writer and performer, I've used quite a few tools over the years to help myself and my clients get unstuck. They fall into three overlapping categories: physical, mental and spiritual. Whether your mind is stuck or running amok, grab the reins and take charge.

❂ **Do something physical.** Get out and walk, breathe deeply. Some people dig in the garden, others swim, sing or pull out the PlayDoh. Some people do the dishes. Keep your body busy and focus on what you're doing. As your mind wanders off into the regrets of the past or throws itself into the fear of the future, gently tug it back to the task at hand and exhale.

❂ **Read something spiritual.** I keep an eight-page booklet in my purse, with just enough information to remind me of the basics, such as, "Your creative process begins with a thought, and the strongest and most creative words are: "I am."

❂ **Write something crazy…or profound.** Amazing things happen when you put your thoughts on paper in a stream-of-consciousness style of writing. Things spill out that you hadn't realized were hiding in there. Now, in the light of day, you'll see they are false beliefs. Let them go, and give yourself a new thought: "I am________." That's where your profound power reveals itself.

❂ **Release something old.** Nobody wins when you wrestle with your thoughts. Step back and observe the old beliefs in your mental chatter, but don't attach to the thoughts or judge them. Simply grab the reins, say goodbye to the old patterns you no longer need, and speak your new thought.

❂ **Discover something new.** Perhaps you're *not* stuck. It may just be the Universe saying to you, "Consider this…"

It's interesting that my improv comedy teacher gave me the same wise messages as the Buddhist monk who led many of my meditation retreats:

❂ When you're stuck, be quiet, observe and listen.

❂ Make a strong choice. There are no mistakes, only choices and consequences.

❂ Walk in knowing who you are and what you want.

❂ Joyfully, actively say "Yes!" to the Universe. Amazing, unimagined things will unfold for you.

❂ Everything is a gift.

❂ Trust in the process. You know more than you think you do.

Whether you're heading into a meeting or an interview that seems formidable, or you're facing those daily doubts that nibble at your self-esteem, your toolbox is essential.

Secrets To Living A Passionate Life

By Janet Bray Attwood

*"There are two great days in a person's life—
the day we are born and the day we discover why."
~William Barclay*

Do you ever feel discouraged and frustrated with your life? Do you ever feel like your dreams will never become reality? Who among us doesn't know living our passion is the key to a happy and fulfilled life?

The trick for many people, though, is figuring out what your passion really is. I've often said, "The number one reason people don't get what they want, is they don't know what they want." Clarity is critical to success. Clarity leads to power—the power to act—which is the basis of achievement, fulfillment and happiness in life. Without a clear direction you are either paralyzed or running around in circles. Worse, you can never reach your full potential, because you dare not fully commit. Not just any direction will do, and therein lies the challenge.

Each of us is unique and has something special to offer the world. To be truly happy we must use our uniqueness to add value to the lives of others.

One day while my business partner Chris Attwood and I were on the phone with our friend and advisor, Bill Levacy, Bill shared with us what I feel is the essence of what's required to create anything you want in your life. It goes like this:

❂ **Intention** Consciously stating what you choose to create in your life is the first step to manifesting it.

❂ **Attention** Your life becomes like that on which you put your attention. Give attention to that which you choose to create in your life, and it will begin to show up.

❂ **No Tension** When you are open to what is appearing in this moment, you allow Universal will to move through you. When you hold tightly to your concepts of how things should be, you shut off the flow of life, which in turn prevents you from enjoying your personal destiny.

So what is personal destiny and do you have one? Of course you do. We all do. Think about it—not one person on the planet is exactly like anyone else. You have your unique gifts, because you have a special role to play in the world which requires giving those gifts. When you're playing that role, you're living your personal destiny. When you are aligned with your destiny, your life is joyful, delightful, exciting and fulfilling.

Your passions are the loves of your life. They are the things which are most deeply important to you. These are the things which, when you're doing them or talking about them, light you up.

What's another clue for living a passionate life? A young girl who collected autographs of famous people was at the airport waiting to board her plane when she saw a crowd of people standing around a small man in a white robe. She knew this man had to be someone well-known because of the large crowd around him. She went up to one of the people standing nearby and asked who the man was. She was told, "That's Maharishi Mahesh Yogi, a great saint from the Himalayas."

The girl excitedly ran up to Maharishi and immediately asked for his autograph. Maharishi took her pen and paper, looked her straight in the eyes and said, "I will give you something much more important than my autograph." And on the piece of paper he wrote one word.

Enjoy.

What was the message Maharishi was conveying? That the whole purpose of life is to enjoy it. When you are not enjoying, you're out of the flow of life. You are missing your purpose.

Again, what's so important about enjoying what you are doing? Think about all the greatest people on the planet, past and present. Every one of them, without exception, loved what they did or are now doing. Every single one of them. Their lives may not have been easy, they certainly faced challenges, and yet, they LOVED what they were doing.

Now think about the people you know who are truly happy. Don't they love what they're doing in their lives? Maybe there are some parts of their lives which are challenging, but when it comes down to it, they love how they spend their days and who they spend their lives with, don't they?

To have absolute success in any area, the most important prerequisite must be that you have a passion for doing it. So do passion and enjoyment go hand in hand? Absolutely. Passion is the inner fire which propels you forward through the combination of love for what you're doing and the inner sense of purpose which comes from connecting to one's deepest passions. Enjoyment arises from this combination of love and purposefulness.

The people whom you love are associated with your passions and, in many cases, your relationship with them may BE your passion. It's not unusual for people to list their spouse or their family or their children among their top passions. For most people, your destiny will be fulfilled as part of a team, and your family is your most fundamental team.

Passion and love are inextricably intertwined, because they both arise from the heart. When you follow your passions, you will love your life. Your passions are not your destiny; they are the clues or keys to your personal destiny. The more passionate your life, the more closely your life is aligned with your destiny.

Destiny is a life's journey. Passions change and morph over time as you come to know and understand yourself more deeply. As you follow your passions, you will find yourself drawn irresistibly onward, until one day you'll wake up and find you are living a passionate life, filled with a sense of destiny.

How To Sing Your Way Out of A Corner

By Olivia Mellan

When I was trying to write my "morning pages" from Julia Cameron's *The Artist's Way*, I realized that, like both my parents, my morning thoughts were lists of my worries and concerns. I was getting sick of writing these worry lists about meeting writing deadlines; worries about whether my headaches were a symptom of something scarily wrong; worries about my kid's well-being, etc., morning after morning.

So I asked myself: How can I use what's coming up for me in a healthier way? The idea of taking my neurotic fears and concerns and writing a spoof song about them came to me, and presto—I started to write a worry list song. Doing that instantly transformed my anxiety through humor into something creative and fun for me and got me out of my anxious state.

This spoof songwriting activity came in handy again recently when I was feeling sad about getting old. I wrote "I Enjoy Being A Crone" in a 15-minute session with myself, and instantly, my feelings about getting older got more positive. My inspirations were: negative feelings about slowing down physically, having trouble losing weight, sleeping poorly, facial wrinkles and noticing my memory was less sharp.

Part of those lyrics (sung to the tune of "I Enjoy Being A Girl" from *Flower Drum Song*) are:

"When I've found a no-fuss hairdo
And found time that is all my own
I float like the clouds on air do
I enjoy being a crone!
When I've spent some time tap dancing
Found some space where I'm all alone
I find my life so entrancing
I enjoy being a crone!
I smile when I think about my friendships
I beam realizing I work less
I kvell meditating on my loved ones
And spend time ridding my life of excess!
I'm truly someone who's grateful
For the life that I call my own
I know well that I have a plate full
I enjoy being a crone!
Instead of a search for meaning
Listening while others piss and moan
Now I nurture the gems I'm gleaning
I enjoy being a crone!
I'm strictly a woman's woman
With a good man to call my own
No more hours spent to please some new
man,
I'm so glad that I'm a crone…
schmoozing with crones… like…. me!

Also, when I was a non-recovering overspender—now I'm recovering—I wrote a spoof song called "When I shop" to "At the Hop" (an oldie rock number by Danny and the Juniors) that helped me look at my imperfections in this area with humor and gentleness and begin to change the pattern.

So my advice for you is to consider infusing some humor and creativity into your anxieties and fears to access a different part of your brain. Listen to some old songs for inspiration and sing your way out of your blues.

What's Your Excuse?

By Oriana Green

Divide your paper into two columns, and in the first one write a list of every single excuse you have ever given yourself about why you have whatever problem you are currently working on. Think back through every stage of your life and examine how you felt about your issue and what limiting things you may have told yourself about it. Try and name 50 or 100 excuses, and be detailed in naming them. For example:

❂ My third grade teacher told me I couldn't draw.

❂ My mother always said I should just get married and not worry about money.

❂ My best friend dismissed every idea I ever had to start my own business.

❂ My first boss belittled all my attempts to contribute ideas to the team.

In the second column, counter each excuse with another viewpoint, listing ways you could and can overcome that self-imposed barrier. For example:

❂ My third grade teacher was not equipped to recognize alternative forms of creative intelligence. I turned out to have a great eye for form and color, which I may pursue in a career as an interior designer. Whether or not I was able to draw a house well at age 8 is not a marker for future success in a creative field. I know I am overflowing with valuable, original ideas.

❂ My mother was speaking from her own narrow experience of life, not from an informed point of view. While I may indeed decide to marry, it is not a solution to any problem—financial or otherwise. I know I do need to take responsibility for my own finances, and I vow to educate myself on that topic so I can escape my mother's prediction and advice.

❂ My best friend was not a successful businesswoman, nor in any position to ridicule my dreams from any place other than her own envy and competitive spirit. I realize my ideas do have worth, and I choose to seek feedback about them only from qualified mentors who can guide me with authentic motives and from a place of true experience.

❂ My first boss was probably jealous of my enthusiasm and drive to better myself and may have put me down in order to maintain her own fragile self-esteem. I now see through that and acknowledge that I did and still do have excellent ideas—I simply need to find the right situations to present them. I no longer allow others' negativity to undermine ideas which I believe to be good.

Refer back to this list often, adding any new excuses you conjure, and be sure to immediately counter them, as well. There is a way around every roadblock you create; you just have to be determined to find it. And the next time you catch yourself clinging to one of your tired excuses, take your own advice from column B and do something differently this time.

No Special Brain Cells Required

By Terri Jiganti Stewart

Maria called somewhat reluctantly to make an appointment. Her divorce attorney required that she take steps toward managing her own finances. Intellectually, she believed it was good advice, but she didn't plan to follow it. Her husband had always managed the money. She had other interests and skills and believed she could never understand investments. In fact her plan was to have her brother make the decisions for her.

When we met I assured her that I'd had the same negative mindset about finances. As an English major, I was certain I wasn't good with numbers. Through an unlikely series of events, I ended up going to business school and earning my MBA. As it turns out, there are no special brain cells required to learning about money and investing! All you need is a little patience and effort to learn the vocabulary of money. What surprised me most was that the subject is interesting. The subject of money and how to manage it is intensely relevant to your life and everyone's life.

So Maria and I started out slowly. I asked her to begin by making no decision at all for a few months. We met three times over the next few months to discuss her situation and then some of the options available to her. Each time, I gave her some material to read so that the subject matter wasn't so intimidating.

Eventually, it was time to make a decision for current and future money management. In order to reduce the stress involved, we started with a small amount of money. After a few months, Maria was able to see how the investment worked and she was ready to invest more of her money. It helped for her to know the pros and cons of each investment and to understand that no investment is perfect. She was always aware of the exit strategy in case she wanted to get out of an investment.

As the years have passed, she has invested her divorce proceeds and some ongoing savings. She has learned quite a bit and makes decisions on her own terms. The fact that she is in control is no longer intimidating. It's now a source of pride.

The Language of Success

By Leah Grant

Successful women use different language than women who are stuck. If you listen closely to what you say and how you say it, you'll receive clues for shifting your focus and popping you into a new mindset. Here are a couple of language shifts to implement.

The "always/never" shift

When you say "always" or "never," such as "I always make mistakes when I use a computer" or "I never get any good leads," you actually shut off the possibility of things happening another way. Always and never are absolutes. If you do something correctly on the computer, you may keep messing with it until something goes wrong, since you're convinced you always make a mistake when using the computer. Or when you are given a great lead, you might toss it aside, convinced it's too good to be true.

When you hear yourself saying "always" or "never," stop yourself and reframe the sentence to allow for more possibilities. Using the examples above, you could say: "I am learning to use the computer better" and "I haven't received any good leads yet." These alternatives shift the brain from an absolute belief to a state of possibility.

As a quick exercise, say the first two sentences, pause then say the second two. Did you notice anything? Most women can feel the difference between them in their bodies.

The "what if" shift

Recently, I was talking to a small business owner at a networking meeting. She shared with me that what stopped her from being successful were her "what ifs." Such as: *What if I don't get any clients?* and *What if my commission check doesn't come in time to pay the rent?* or *What if no one buys my product?* plus several more equally dire worries. She said she couldn't stop thinking about all the "what ifs."

I suggested that instead of eliminating them, she merely shift to thinking about positive "what ifs" rather than negative ones. If your brain creates "what ifs," put it to work generating questions like: *What if I get an order for 200 units?* or *What if I get paid double what I was expecting?* or *What if I had more leads than I could follow-up on by myself?*

She loved that she didn't have to change or stop a process that was already in motion. She only needed to shift to *positive* possibilities.

So what could happen if you shifted to success language?

The "I can't" shift

Most of the time you say "I can't" you're lying. When you say "I can't get a raise" or "I can't make more money" or "I can't speak in public," you're lying. Think about it. You *could* get a raise or make more money if you either asked for one, changed jobs or got promoted. What you may have meant was "I didn't get a raise" or 'I'm too afraid to ask for more money." Likewise, if your life depended on it, you could get on a stage with a microphone and say something. It might not be eloquent, but you *could* do it.

When you use the phrase "I can't" it has the same limiting effect as "always" and "never." There is no option for you to achieve your goal in the future. You are stating that you've given up. You are announcing yourself as a victim.

Focus instead on what you *can* do and use language that tells the truth. For example, if a boss hands you a project and tells you he needs it by Friday, instead of saying: "I can't do that" say "I can get you the first part of the proposal by that deadline. If you'd like all of it, I need you to re-assign the other projects I'm responsible for this week."

An added benefit of eliminating "I can't" from your vocabulary is that you'll feel and appear stronger.

The "have to" shift

I had a client who used the phrase "have to" in almost every sentence one day when she called for our session. She said, "I have to feed the kids" and "I have to pick up my dry cleaning" and "I have to finish reading that report."

I asked her what would happen if she didn't do those things. Would the sky fall? Would she go to work naked? What would *really* happen if she didn't do those things?

She admitted that not much would happen. Her kids were old enough to fend for themselves from the cupboards if they got hungry enough, she had plenty of clothes in her closet, and the meeting covering the report was the following afternoon.

The reality is, there are very few things you have to do in life. Saying “I have to” ignores that you have a choice. It places you in the role of being driven by your life, rather than you being in the driver’s seat. I encourage my clients to embrace the choices they have, and not to give them away in the language they use.

Try one more quick exercise

Say: “I have to prepare for the new client meeting on Friday.” **Then say:** “I have chosen to prepare for the new client meeting on Friday.”

Isn’t it amazing what a difference to your attitude adding one small word can have?

There are many more language shifts you can make that will propel you out of being stuck. Once you become more aware of the words you’re using, you’ll begin to notice the words other people choose as well.

Four Inside Changes

By Sharon Olson

Henry David Thoreau said, "The smallest seed of faith is better than the largest fruit of happiness." When I reach a point of feeling stuck in my life, the feeling can be terrifying and seem endless. I lose faith and can become anxious. But in reflecting on these periods, I realize they provide a great opportunity for change and growth. The fact that I feel stuck and want to correct this feeling is actually the thing that propels me into movement.

We can all be bothered by outside forces we can't change. I sometimes remind myself that I can't change certain external factors, such as: whether I am going to get the deal, the performance of the stock market or interest rate changes. But I *can* change internal factors and how I perceive my condition.

When you look at four aspects of your life—mental, physical, social and spiritual—you can create movement in each area with these methods.

❂ **Mental:** Take an accounting of things that are going right in your life and remember to give thanks. This mental exercise of sorts is a good way to keep a grateful heart.

❂ **Physical:** Physical exercise releases natural endorphins into your system to lift your mood and increase energy.

❂ **Social:** When you are stuck in business, ask yourself this question: If you had to start all over again in another city, what would you do to grow your business? When you have answered that question, set off to carry out those tasks. This helps to open up your thinking and connect with new people and ideas. I call it "getting in there and wiggling a little."

❂ **Spiritual:** Although life can be dark at times, realize that within yourself lies the power to transform your own experiences. Your star can shine only when it's seen against the backdrop of darkness.

The Answers Are All In There!

By Stacey Lane

Fear is probably the most common thing that gets people stuck. And one of the worst ways fear sabotages you is tricking you into deciding your goals aren't really worth pursuing. You may have thought about pursuing your dream more than once, only to come up with plenty of excuses why it's a bad idea.

Think back over goals, or even ideas, that you've discarded. Chances are, fear played a role in why you didn't move forward. Fears that keep us stuck can be seductive—they usually sound rational, practical and oh-so responsible.

So try something different the next time you've got a goal or idea you want to pursue. Write it down. Then monitor your thoughts about the goal or idea you've written down. Notice all of the different thoughts or excuses you have about the goal. Write them all down under your goal, leaving space between each excuse. Then deconstruct each excuse to reveal the truth behind it.

For example, if your idea is to quit your secure job to do something that you feel more passionate about, some of the excuses you come up with might be:

- I don't know where to start.
- I'll never make enough money.
- It's a tough job market.
- I've got too many obligations to do something like this.

❂ How will I know if this is the right thing?

Analyze those excuses to see what's real about them and what's not. The practical concerns are easily solvable; it's the emotional excuses that need the most study. "It's a tough job market" may reflect issues of self-confidence. If you're honest with yourself, you'll probably discover there are many success stories of people who have successfully changed careers—in even tougher job markets. If this one still stops you, try finding people who have been successful and ask them for advice.

The excuse "I'll never make enough money" speaks to the fears we all have about financial security. But instead of letting that fear stop you, think of a practical approach. Develop a budget so you are crystal clear about your financial obligations. You also might brainstorm some unconventional career transition strategies to help bridge the gap from where you are to where you want to be. For example, you might negotiate flexible hours at work so you have more time to pursue your passion. Taking action in the direction of your goal or idea, no matter how small the step might be, counteracts the excuse.

Then there's "How will I know if this is the right thing?" This is an all-purpose excuse you give yourself in desperation, just in case the long list of other excuses can't stop your idea or goal. Have you wasted time in the past on pursuits that didn't pan out? Perhaps those need analyzing to see what patterns of self-sabotage might have been at work there. This excuse also masks fear of success—if your idea does work, then you'll be committed to actually doing it every month, which might lead to all kinds of other opportunities to stretch your self-image.

There is always another layer behind emotional excuses, and you can train yourself to spot this negative thinking when it first pops up—and evaluate it objectively. The good news is, if you do decide to move forward with a goal after going through this process, you should have much more confidence in your idea and more enthusiasm to pursue it.

From Force to FLOW!

By Tamra Fleming

You may have noticed times in your life when the amount of effort you put forth did not produce the desired outcome. By trying too hard, you instead seemed to be more effective at creating your own roadblocks to success. Pushing, straining, struggling, trying and working harder may all seem like the right ways to accomplish your goals. Yet, time after time, you may find these strategies just don't work.

What does it mean to switch from Force to FLOW? It may run counter to your training and experience to step back, pause and stop trying so hard to force your will upon a situation. Stepping into FLOW means: giving up control; seeking others for external feedback; working creatively and playfully; and trusting the wondrous wisdom of your higher self and others.

Recognizing different types of energies

The energy of Force is draining and exhausting; it depletes creativity and ultimately blocks FLOW. When work gets bogged down, creativity disappears into the ether. When you attempt to induce Providence, you actually strip away its fantastic power. This frantic grasping disintegrates the energy of FLOW—and creates a result that is the *opposite* of what you hope for.

Conversely, the empowering energy of FLOW—filled with uplifting qualities like joy and curiosity—leads you to success in unexpected, often delightful ways.

1st column: **Symptoms of the energy of Force**
2nd column: **Characteristics of the energy of FLOW**

accusation	support
anxiety	calm
assumption	openness
blame	delight
destruction	construction
distrust	trust
dwelling on negative	seeing the positive
effort	effortless
excessive preparation	faith
expectations	anticipation
fear	joy
frustration	wonder
judgment	devotion
mind tricks	creativity
obsessing	exploration
perfection	flexibility
pressure	relaxation
resistance	letting go
rigidity	balance
separation	discovery
vigilance	curiosity

Results of the energy of Force include:

Anger
Broken dreams
Disappointment
Disharmony
Dissatisfaction
Distrust
Failure

Lack of confidence

Results of the energy of FLOW include:

Bliss
Unexpected benefits
Satisfaction
Harmony
Ease
Synergy
Surprising successes
Confidence

A lot happens when you're not actively doing and pursuing. The energy of progress is fueled by release. It is, in a sense, working *smarter*, not harder.

For example, this past year I set out to launch my life's dream in the form of a creative and dynamic website. With the vision clear, I assembled a talented team and we began to work hard to make it happen. With underlying beliefs such as "life is hard" and perfectionist expectations, the project began to flounder rather than flourish. The more Force was applied to the situation, the further the dream retreated from manifestation. Intense effort and expectations resulted in the breakdown of the website and sent the team into blame, anger and frustration. Communication blocks increased, while energy and enthusiasm decreased.

The result of a project centered in the energy of Force was a website filled with blocks in FLOW, and challenges that could have been easily avoided.

But all was not lost. As a team, we were able to take a step back (out of the energy of Force) and assess what had happened. Pausing to take stock of the situation, we could easily see how the energy of anxiety and fear had almost strangled our hopes and dreams. Stepping into FLOW allowed us to gain much-needed perspective and access a host of supportive, knowledgeable resources. New solutions and creative ideas surfaced. With a new plan our team gained renewed energy and enthusiasm.

By adopting the attitude that "life is easy," the project shifted, allowing the original vision to surface…a *joy* for all involved!

So how can *you* shift from the habit of tightening your grip to the practice of loosening your grasp?

❂ **Identify:** Recognize and move past an unproductive approach to the problem you believe you're currently facing. When the energy of Force appears, recognize the pattern immediately—be it agitation, irritation or an unwillingness to let go—and STOP!

It's easy to miss the clues telling us it's time to stop and let go. By pushing to control and taking care of everything, we become strained and frustrated. As active, successful women, we know how to get things done. This is part of our nature and has its place in the overall picture. But when we have done all that needs doing, it's time to *stop*. Let go of the need to fix, check, control, etc. Practice deep breathing. Slow down. Change your setting to help break the pattern—step outside for a brisk five-minute walk. Consciously and willingly let go of the patterns of Force and welcome the energies of FLOW.

❂ **Retreat, reflect, release:** Now take a step back and look at the big picture from all angles. Get a fresh perspective. Make sure you're not "missing the forest for the trees." Give yourself space. Let go of deadlines, "shoulds" and "the rules." Break the rules! Change your focus. Revel in the mystery of the unknown. Get excited about what's next. Allow what you need and desire to surface and appear in unexpected, new or transformed ways. Release your tension physically, mentally and even spiritually.

❂ **Get creative:** Tap into your feminine energy and power. Creativity is at the very core of femininity—it's a most powerful tool. Creativity is FLOW.

❂ **Connect to potentiality:** Anything is possible! "Where there's a will, there's a way." Take action without Force. When you change your perspective, the problem or issue at hand shifts as well.

❂ **Gather ideas from everywhere:** Open up your eyes and ears to new avenues and resources. Interview others: friends, family, colleagues, professionals, even neighbors and acquaintances. Research books, magazines, TV shows, the Internet, etc. Broaden your horizons.

❂ **Break down the tasks ahead of you:** Don't overwhelm yourself. Just take the next obvious steps and keep moving forward (with plenty of curiosity and openness).

And remember, the cliché rings true: Never give up! Keep stepping, keep walking, keep moving and keep going! May the FLOW be with You.

The Empty Chair

By Susan Bross

When a client reports that something is holding her back, and I'm not sure what it might be, I use the Empty Chair technique. I move an empty chair into her line of sight, and then ask her to close her eyes. I use some basic visualizing techniques to get her relaxed, ask her to pay attention to her breathing, etc., until I know she's relaxed. Then we begin.

Visualize the empty chair in your mind, and in that chair visualize the self who has already reached the goal you're trying to reach and has comfortably achieved what you want. Thank your successful self for coming and observe what it feels like to have that problem solved. Now in your mind's eye, change chairs with your successful self, and notice what it feels like to be that successful self and what feels different.

Now that you know what it feels like to be that successful self, imagine that self has a gift for you, wrapped beautifully in gold paper with a shiny bow. The successful self gives you this present, because it is what you need to reach where you want to go. In opening the gift, the gold of the wrapping and the glow of the bow become one with the shining gift inside, and the golden glow fills you with strength, peace and competence.

You now know without a doubt that you are complete. Sit with this glow of completeness, and when you feel ready, with your mind's eye look at the chair opposite you. The chair is now empty because the successful self is now fully integrated into you, and this integration is the completeness you were searching for. Be one with that completeness, describe it and enjoy it, until you feel at peace. When you are ready, listen again to your breath, and bring that peace and completeness with you as you re-enter the room by opening your eyes.

Then, after asking permission, I ask what was in the gift, and often the client knows exactly what was in the present she received. This confirms for me that so often people know exactly what they require, and need only evoke it in a receiving frame of mind.

❂ Liberally adapted from an exercise I learned from an old professor of mine, Dr. Fred Waddell, who created Solution Focused Financial Coaching, and from whom I've taken much wisdom over the years.

Just Say No

By Meredyth Hunt

Life is full. Full of opportunities to say "yes" to the wonderful things we want and activities we love, as well as "no" to the things we don't want and activities that drain our energy.

Just how many times have you heard the "Don't be a people-pleasing nice girl" speech? And yet I bet you are still overloaded with people wanting your attention and projects needing your expertise that don't contribute positively to your goals or well-being. Right?

You probably say "yes" to things that don't serve you to avoid the uncomfortable feelings that go along with saying "no." And that's a perfect recipe for getting stuck doing all kinds of things that don't move you closer to your goals.

In order to access your life force energy and use it to make your life work, instead of sacrificing it to make someone else's life work, you have to surrender to the stomach-churning fear of saying "no."

The question to ask yourself in any situation is: Does this serve me? If the answer is "no" and you do it anyway, you are sacrificing your own success. Just begin by noticing every day how many large and small ways you sacrifice your time and energy. Do you do extra errands or tasks for others because it's easier than arguing about it? Do you fear being labeled as uncooperative, lazy or petty for refusing to help? Do you let your kids drain you to the point that you never have any time for yourself?

There's nothing wrong with wanting an inner life, with your own dreams and goals—and some time to pursue them. Learning to say "no" can free up all the time you need to do just that. But until you can say "no" whenever you want to, then "yes" means nothing. When you can say "no" and work through the feelings of fear and guilt that come up afterward—at least at first—then you'll find all sorts of opportunities will come knocking, because you'll actually have the energy to open the door and receive them.

Income Goals: A Tale of Expecting More (and Buying A Fabulous Couch)

By Mikelann Valterra

Of all the goals women set, one of the most important is how much money they want to earn. Surprisingly, many successful women do not have a specific goal around income. They go through their lives and careers wishing they made more money, but this diffuse desire doesn't seem to translate to earning more.

Why not? For one thing, when you walk around saying, "I need to make more money!" and don't attach a specific amount to this desire, it can translate into free-floating anxiety. Just saying "I want to make more" rarely helps. Goal setting 101 tells us to get specific about our goals and have a timeline. But when it comes to setting earning goals, this can be very difficult.

When you come up with an exact income goal, you give the mind something precise to fix on. The mind loves specific challenges and immediately sets to work problem solving, analyzing and getting creative. When we do not have a specific number to work with, it is difficult to tap into our creativity to accomplish a goal.

But if you have a specific income goal, my question to you is this: Is your number high enough? Study after study tells us that women expect less money from the very beginning. We expect and are satisfied with less money from our employers and pay ourselves less in the world of self-employment.

Yet women tend to be great advocates for those around them. We support our friends in making more money. We counsel them to raise their rates or ask for a raise. But when it comes to looking at ourselves, we often have a blind spot.

So here's a hot suggestion. If you are setting, or assessing your income goal, do two things before you decide on your goal. First, spend some time on the Internet researching what other people get paid to do what you do. Start with www.salary.com, though there are many great Internet sites. I've sat with many women who were shocked to find out they were underpaid for what they did.

Second, use your network. Talk to five different people about income. While friends and colleagues may be reticent to share what they make (though some will share), tell them what you are doing, or thinking of doing, and ask them: "If you were me, how much should I ask for? What do you think this should pay?" One of our greatest strengths as women is our wonderful network. So use it!

A client of mine was deciding on a new income goal. She had wanted to make more money for a while but felt stuck. She made $55,000 and felt she should be making more for what she did. After spending a couple of hours on the Internet researching rates, she was shocked by the median salaries listed for similar job descriptions. She hadn't realize just how underpaid she was.

She then took three colleagues out to coffee and asked for advice on what she should be paid. By the time she talked to several people, she was steaming. But she used this anger to fuel her. She set an income goal of $65,000 and gave herself 18 months to get there. She knew this might entail switching companies and some tough negotiating.

During this time, she fell in love with a beautiful but very expensive couch in a furniture boutique downtown. She decided the couch would be her reward. Once she reached her goal, she would celebrate by buying it. More than once during negotiations, she went to the boutique and sat on the couch, thinking about her goal. Perseverance won over, and a year later she was making $65,000 with a promising career in front of her. And the couch looks fabulous in her house!

Find a specific reward for when you reach your goal. Years ago, when I started my private practice, I set an income goal and decided that when I reached it, I would celebrate by buying myself an expensive gold bracelet. There were many times I thought about that bracelet while marketing and building my business. I did hit the goal and spent $300 on a gorgeous bracelet that I wear to this day as a personal reminder to me of achieving a goal.

It's possible to get unstuck when it comes to making more money. To get unstuck and back on the road to success, set a specific income goal, make sure it's high enough and then reward yourself well when you've accomplished it. Here's to greater abundance!

Duct Tape and WD40

By Chellie Campbell

Someone shared with me that all of life's problems can be solved with two things—duct tape and WD40. (For those of you who never get your hands dirty, WD40 is a spray-on lubricant that loosens lug nuts and other stuck things.) If it moves and it shouldn't, you need duct tape. And if it doesn't move and it should, you need WD40. That's a great image for life. You need duct tape to keep you on purpose—to stick to your guns, stick to your ideals, stick to your goals. You need WD40 to get you up and moving—to get out of bed, off to the gym, to propel you out of the box.

Distinguishing when you need to use duct tape and when you need to use WD40 is the tricky part. Many businesses have failed because they didn't see a new product or technology on the rise and stuck to the old way of doing things, playing it safe. Just like food kept long past its expiration date, sometimes people stay in jobs, neighborhoods or relationships beyond their fruitfulness. When the ship is sinking, it's appropriate to jump ship! You don't have to go down with it.

Then again, it's sometimes best to use that duct tape and stay the course—you don't want to give up on your dream just before it's fulfilled. Maybe the next ship you send out is the one that will bring home the treasure, so you have to know when to heed the cry: "Don't give up the ship!"

The creator of the copier machine took his new invention to Kodak first. The copier is a kind of camera, so it seemed a natural connection.

However, the Kodak executives rejected it—after all, they had better quality photographic equipment already. They just didn't see the business application of the invention. So the inventor went to Xerox, and today that's why we Xerox documents rather than Kodak them. The Kodak executives had too much duct tape holding them to their known business model—they needed a squirt or two of WD40 to rouse them to act on a new idea. The inventor had plenty of WD40, which helped him create a new business machine, and enough duct tape to refuse to give up in the face of rejection.

How do you know "when to hold 'em and when to fold 'em," to use the famous poker analogy? You use the duct tape and stick to your goals as long as you passionately believe in them and are committed to making them happen, when you enjoy the pursuit of the dream, whether or not it is realized and when your intuition tells you to keep going. And most of all, when you know that you will succeed, because you're willing to do whatever it takes to make it happen.

Behind every so-called overnight sensation there were years of study, failed attempts, more learning, small successes and dogged persistence. Lots of duct tape. It looks messy, like a first-grader's taped-together construction paper project. Succeed or fail, your passion and commitment to your purpose will be the WD40 that moves and inspires you to get up each day, excited about the new possibilities today will bring. If you enjoy your dream and all the steps along the way, you'll be a success every day of your life.

Tear It Up!
By Nikki Kilgore

OK, so you feel stuck, overwhelmed. Perhaps the problem or issue is complicated, or maybe you have many issues facing you. Whatever it is, you are feeling stuck.

First, take a full piece of paper (or start a new document if you prefer to do it on a computer) and list *all* the things that are bothering you (related or unrelated to the issue). Write down all your problems, obstacles, etc., leaving a good bit of space between each one. Then give it a once over. Is there anything else missing or nagging at you? (If you did it on a computer, print it out.)

Next, take that piece of paper and tear it so you have each item or problem on its own scrap of paper. The act of tearing the paper gives you a feeling of satisfaction and taking control, which also drives home the idea that you really are physically separating these items from each other.

Now that you have each item on its own piece of paper, you can deal with it. You can prioritize, handle, complete, delegate, put aside or perhaps let go of it all together. It is amazing how doable each obstacle is when you deal with it individually.

Take your new pile of individual issues and put them in order of importance. You can only deal with one at a time anyway. Then handle the one on top. Ignore the rest, until you decide something has become a priority.

The point is, you must separate each problem so it can be removed from the morass—

and then the morass disappears! When multiple worries, concerns and issues are all glommed together like a stew of problems, it can be overwhelming and difficult to address the individual or the whole. Remember—create bite-sized pieces and manageable chunks.

When you don't separate the different items or components, you often end up playing the "shell game" with another person or with yourself. I've seen this with so many friends and clients. They state their problem, I offer some ideas and solutions and they say, "Yes, but..." and proceed to tell me about another problem. So I switch my attention to answering that one, but then they bring up another point, and so on and so on. They try to keep shifting their focus and never really address any issue. We do this to ourselves all the time, especially if we leave things in our heads rather than getting them out on paper.

So, get it down on paper. Then tear it up!

Bring Out Your Own Brilliance

By Deborah Buchta

In mentoring women leaders, one of the most critical things I have learned about breaking through barriers, is not to try and do it alone. Through a process I call *flocreation*™, one of the fundamental principles of creating more flow in your life is to create a supportive community. A group of people come together to support one another in expressing their brilliance and talking openly and compassionately about their blocks.

Each of us has a unique gift to bring to the world, which I call our *brilliance*—the innate talent, knowledge, skillfulness or aptitude that beckons us to creative callings that enrich the lives of others, the planet and ourselves. When brilliance is released and set into motion with action and collaborative support, powerful transformation occurs in our lives and the world.

Your community, which could be one person or several, is extremely important in providing an ongoing support and feedback system. Your community members also hold each other accountable in taking the steps towards their visions, as well as cheer each other's successes. They believe in you and remind you of your vision when you get off track.

They hold a field of potentiality for you, as you do for them. I call this a *brilliance community*—a reflective field in which you can see and embody your own brilliance through the eyes of others. When you can see and support the unique gifts of others, you are able to see your own. This is a community of like-minded people who desire deep connection with others through positive feedback and true collaboration, while releasing their old beliefs of competition and jealousy or "not enough for me."

Through your community, you receive opinion-free feedback in a safe environment, where the intention is that everyone is supported in achieving their visions and releasing their blocks. When you desire the best for others and help them get what they desire, you are laying the groundwork for receiving what you desire.

Your brilliance community thrives in a field of potentiality, an environment of unlimited potential that requires you to hold a clear vision of your own potential and also see the unlimited potential of others. Holding the field of potentiality is a positive circular energy—you see others and others reflect you.

Many times we get stuck because we're having trouble breaking old patterns in our thinking and self-imposed limitations. This is an opportunity to use your community to "bust your caps," which means stepping up to the next level of your capabilities and raising your self-image by releasing self-imposed limitations. This allows you to see yourself in a new way and to focus on your brilliance rather than your flaws. When we can only see ourselves through our limitations, it blocks us from our true capabilities and achieving who we can become. We often do negative self-talk and harbor thoughts such as, "I'm not good enough, smart enough or I don't belong."

Instead, imagine we have layers of caps (limitations) stacked on our heads, and each time we release or pop off a cap, we can have a new and improved self-image.

The process of Flocreation™ is a mindset and a way of being. It's about practicing limitless potential, experiencing unconstrained creativity and extending ourselves into our infinite brilliance.

My Top Ten Ways To Get Unstuck

By Selma Lewis, Ph.D.

One of the biggest obstacles to getting unstuck is recognizing you *are* stuck. This sounds almost silly, but your brain can fool you into sinking day by day into unhealthy patterns and putting up with what should be intolerable.

The human brain has evolved over time. The good news is that it has allowed us to flourish all over the earth, create language arts and cultures that are dazzling. The bad aspect is that evolution seems to favor repetition of thoughts, behaviors and emotions. It's as if our brain believes everything we once did has survival value and we should do that again and again. We missed the saber tooth tiger by avoiding the lake at nighttime, so we never go to the lake.

I bet you know what I mean. Maybe you took a job, telling yourself it was temporary until you could afford college or go after the exciting career in a different city. Or perhaps, like many women, you helped a boyfriend or husband get ahead in his career, while you put your desires on hold—all while whispering to yourself, "Someday" (which has never come). Neuroscientists would say you developed the chemistry or habit of waiting to begin your real life. Perhaps you have a hidden passion or talent you want to develop, but you feel fear, so you hesitate, procrastinate or find good deeds that need doing so you can postpone pursuing your goal. The bigger your dream, the more fear you may experience.

Below you'll find ten tips for getting unstuck, but the first is my favorite way—a guided imagery experience.

1. It's best to read this a few times and then close your eyes and create the imagery. After a few moments the dream-like fantasy will take you on an inner journey. Even better, record this and listen to it on a headset with your eyes shut. Do it as slowly as possible. Don't try to multi-task, as you will only cheat yourself. Give yourself the gift of a few minutes of complete focus.

Get comfortable where you are sitting or lying. Close your eyes. Take three deep breaths. Pause often to feel everything in the scene with all your senses.

Imagine you are walking along a beach on a perfect day. Feel the sun warm your body just the right amount. Allow the warmth to penetrate your skin, relaxing you more deeply with each breath. Feel you body become limp and heavy with comfort. Smell the sea air, listen to the sounds of the waves gently breaking and other sounds of the beach. Feel the sand as you walk along. Notice if you are walking down near the water where the sand is wet and cool or in hot, dry sand. Allow your body to relax; feel your shoulders drop.

Begin remembering a favorite vacation and how relaxed your body can feel. Imagine having all the time in the world for this walk, enjoying your senses. As you stroll along the beach, you see a treasure chest half buried in the sand. You drop down and begin to dig.

The faster you dig, the more excited you become. You uncover it, and take a moment to visually explore it. You once believed in magic, and as you examine this chest, you know in your deepest self it is a magical tool.

As you open the chest, you spy an object that has a message meant just for you about your next step toward your goal. Some people find a note, or a genie in a glass bottle or an inner guide. It doesn't matter. You may know exactly what the message means, or you may need to dream with it tonight as you sleep. Your unconscious never fails to communicate.

When you are ready, you can symbolically take the message with you, or you can leave it there. Thank yourself and the universe for this gift of self-knowledge. Return to where you were sitting and stretch a few moments.

Before you forget, write down as much of this inner journey as you can. Make a sketch. Say the message over a few times and write it clearly. Reread this before you sleep tonight.

2. Imagine you are your younger self, age 10 or so. Feel your feet on the ground as you run to go play. Spend a few moments doing an activity you loved as a child. Feel the size of your body, and especially notice your energy and vitality. Breathe in and out a few times, and allow your body to fill with more and more energy. Take an inner snapshot, including feeling this vast amount of energy that is yours. Picture yourself in your daily life now having this much energy, and see yourself take a first step toward your goal.

3. Get up and go outside right now. Jump from one square of sidewalk to another. Or over a gutter filled with running water. Or set up an obstacle course and jump, leap and hop from one to the next. Curl your lips into a smile, even if you feel resistant. Before long you will be ready to do what has you stuck.

4. Get up right now and go clean out a small drawer in your house or the backseat of your car. It doesn't matter what you choose, just begin some physical activity. As you get into it, you can easily transfer that energy to what has you stuck. Getting started is often the hardest moment.

5. I often get stuck when I have to write something such as this. I pretend I'm talking to a friend, and say out loud what occurs to me without inner editing. I will write or record my words and then sit at the computer and input that beginning. From there, I usually have no trouble continuing. Sometimes I call a friend (who is nonjudgmental and caring) and begin to brainstorm with her, which jumpstarts my ideas, and then I can continue by myself.

6. For writing projects where I feel stuck—the inner critic is fully engaged—I open a book or magazine, not necessarily on a topic even related, and begin to read. Within a few moments, my back burner brain has an idea, and I catch it, stop reading and get into the writing.

7. If you feel stuck in life itself, remember back to a time when you felt free and flowing. Allow the feeling to build within you as you remember more and more about that time. See what you were doing, what you wore, how you spent your time, what excited you, what you were wanting. Recall how you trusted your inner self and direction. Even now you still have that in you. Now sense what is different in your life. What is keeping you stuck? Can you imagine a magical way of transforming that? For example, you may feel all the obligations and responsibilities of your life that you believe prevent you from starting a new career or moving to a new location. Imagine all those situations as giant boulders keeping you from going forward. Magically allow yourself to be strong enough to get through, either by yourself or with an army of magical animal helpers. Ask your inner wisdom to help you find an image to use. You might need to sit for a half hour daily for a few weeks and play inwardly until you get just the right image. Don't give up. Exaggerate it for a moment. How do you feel?

8. Call a friend and brainstorm how to get unstuck, and make a specific and concrete list of small steps to move you toward change. Write them out on a large sheet of paper and post it somewhere you'll always see it. Commit to do these things by a certain date and to check in with your friend. Make yourself accountable as if you were at work.

9. Break old habits. Start to do some new things. Take an alternate route to familiar places. Sit in a different chair when you talk on the phone. Eat in a different restaurant. Take up a hobby. Don't repeat your familiar tales of woe, especially when you're with good friends. Choose what you say with mindfulness about your meaning, and act as if you are a sociologist watching yourself when talking with friends. We redefine ourselves each time we talk.

10. Other times when I'm stuck on a writing project, I go somewhere with minimal distractions: a café, my office (which has no chores or media distractions), a park or similar place. When faced with a dearth of self-imposed diversions—like no oven that suddenly needs cleaning or closet calling for overhaul—I miraculously become productive.

There's No Need To Go It Alone

By Sharon I. Beitzell

Do you have a coach and/or mentor? If not, why? All successful athletes, entertainers and public figures know the value of a coach, whether personal or professional. Coaches can show you how to get you to the top of your game and stay there.

Choosing the right coach/mentor is critical. First I had to realize I needed one. Then came the task of finding the right person for me. I narrowed my focus to two important areas I wanted to improve: presentation content and presentation skills. Since it was difficult to find one person who specialized in my field who could help me with both goals, I choose two coaches.

My coaches are people I highly respect, are successful in their field with a proven track record and highly respected by their peers. As coaches, girlfriends don't count! While girlfriends are great listeners, sympathizers and our biggest fans, there are times we need the brutal truth. Our friends don't want to hurt our feelings.

Coaches help you identify your skill set and build upon them. As a business professional, I have hit many barriers and ruts. If we keep doing the same activity, getting the same results and can't understand why we are not growing, we're in a rut. Activity should not be confused with productivity. When this happens, we lose our focus.

If you haven't written down your goals, I would encourage you to do so. They are the blueprints to your success. Each step you take, go back to the blueprint and ensure the step is moving you closer to your goal, not away from it. When I hit a barrier or rut, it's because I've deviated from the blueprint.

My coach and I have defined weekly, monthly and yearly goals. We have a plan. My coach holds me accountable and helps narrow my focus to stay the course. My goals are written, definable and—yes—achievable. Most important, my coach has taught me to focus my focus.

Share your goals and dreams with those who believe in you. Surround yourself with positive people, so when you get off track or hit a rut they can cheer you when you need it most. Girlfriends do make excellent cheerleaders. Then do something for yourself you will never regret: hire a professional coach.

Create A Road Map for Your Future

By Sue Bates

Sometimes people get stuck simply because they lack clarity. Here is one of the fun ways I help people get in touch with who they are and what they really want. First, list ALL the things in your life that you have always wanted to do or have or be. For example: be a mom, a CEO, a dancer or own a BMW. This will probably be a long list!

Next, go through the list and assign a number between one and ten to indicate how important each item is to you now. Perhaps becoming a ballet dancer is no longer that important. Maybe it rates a two. But you look at having children and you get a strong pull that won't let you go. That would earn a ten. Ask yourself about every item on your list: Does it still have a pull for you? Do you still have a connection to it? It may take a few days to take the time to assess them all. Don't rate them in order of importance, just how strong your urge is for each item right now.

Then, using everything from your list that you ranked an eight and above, create a collage of all these unrealized dreams. Use a large poster board and cut out words and images from magazines or download pictures from the Internet. Google Image Search is a great, fast resource for finding a representation of virtually anything. Then simply paste something to symbolize each of your desires onto the board.

This is such a fun way to really discover who you are and what calls to you, because it uses your right brain. I've seen many of them, and they are all so different—the collages give us a road map to who we really are and what we really want. Create one with several of your friends, so you can see how unique we all are and how the collage really does reveal our individualism.

People tend to get busy and do only what they're supposed to do or should do and they don't take time to really see and listen to who they are. When you have finished your collage, place it where you can see it frequently. Studying it can help refine your dreams and guide you to choose which items on your list you want to pursue the most, which will get things moving in that direction and propel you toward manifesting your goals.

Can't See A Way Out? Get A Bigger Picture

By Oriana Green

These days, many of us spend way too much of our time anchored to our computers, as well as tethered to increasingly smaller screens and devices. It's easy to believe that everything that matters, that drives us, resides inside these machines. The more time we spend with them, the more value we have to assign to them in order to justify the amount of time we devote to them.

All that can lead to a myopic view of life. We can become so involved in our problems that we miss all the many options hovering just beyond our limited view.

Whenever I feel stuck on a problem I see no solution to, I know to change my focus. First I look out my windows. Just changing my focal length reduces eyestrain. I've learned the hard way to always situate my office in a space with expansive views and to make sure I can enjoy them from my desk. There are sacrifices I've made to live far from any city, but one payoff is the eagles I get to watch glide by my windows. Their effortless flight and apparent joy riding the updrafts feed my soul all day long.

Next, I step away from my computer (which is where most of my problems start and end). I go outside and take in the full expanse of my view. If time allows, I settle into my Adirondack chair and feel my tensions ease. Then I deliberately stare at the sky. Not the trees or birds or islands, but just the sky. I try to make my mind go as blank as a cloudless June sky.

What I've found is that I think differently when I look at a big blank canvas like the sea or a lake or the sky. Some days it's a large swath of grass in a park that will clear my mind. I just know that so many more things seem possible when I open up to large vistas.

After I feel I've relaxed into the vacant space, I allow ideas to seep back into my consciousness. I don't actively try to solve my problem. Instead, I take a notebook and jot down whatever thoughts come to me. I prefer to write by hand, because it feels like a more direct connection to my mind. If I don't force the process, more often than not, new approaches to my problem do indeed surface. This technique can also be used for brainstorming sessions and exploding writer's block.

Another way I apply this concept is on long drives. Since it's a 40-mile round trip to the nearest grocery store, all of my drives are long! So I've had lots of practice at this. To relieve the monotony of driving the same roads all the time, I give my mind an assignment for each trip—something to plan or perhaps a problem to solve, and I pull out of my driveway with that firm intention.

As the miles go by and the road curves around bays and along rivers, my mind again responds to the wider views. Soon my ideas are flowing. There is something hypnotic about driving—the movement, the rhythms, the hum of the engine—that always triggers a flood of ideas.

Give it a try on your next car trip. How you capture your ideas is up to you. Dictate them into a pocket recorder; leave yourself voice mail; pull over and take notes or wait until you reach your destination to write them down. Of course, being a passenger in a car or train would be ideal—then you could note your ideas as they unspool from your newly rested mind.

So the next time you find yourself hunched over your keyboard enmeshed in some mental challenge, go find a big piece of sky and wrap your mind up in it.

Working with A Difficult Boss

By Dee Soder, Ph.D.

Study after study has found a high percentage of bad bosses in corporate America. You have to learn to work with difficult people, including bosses, if you want to break through and move ahead. Many people, especially women, get stuck because they are unable to work well with someone they don't respect or like. Chances are that you will work for a bad boss sometime—if you don't already. Even good bosses don't always have time to explain their reasons.

Accordingly, there will be many times you disagree with your boss and can't persuade him or her to change their view. This is easier if you remember that your boss is right—even when he or she is wrong. It's easier if you like your boss to say, "You got it—I'm on it" or "Right away." But unless it is an ethical or legal matter, remember there is a time to salute. Much has been written about bosses, but these five tips will enable you to move beyond your issues in the majority of circumstances.

Five best tips for managing your boss

1. Don't try to change him—you can't!

2. Try to see the world from her perspective. (Beware the "I" mentality—this is the way I would do it…). If you think you have a bad boss, he or she probably thinks you are a problem employee.

3. Remember what makes a bad boss for one person is not necessarily true for another.

4. Be alert to your boss's work style, and beware of people under stress. Remember dominant traits are even more pronounced if the person is stressed. For example, the detail-oriented boss will become a micro-manager under stress.

5. Communicating is vital. Keep your boss informed and don't hesitate to ask questions. Be sure to tell your boss when you've achieved something. Your boss generally won't know you've done something great unless you tell him or her. It is only inappropriate if you've said it badly. Plus your boss wants to know about your accomplishments, too. Why? So she can tell *her* boss.

Rekindling the Spark: From Burned Out To Fired Up Again

By Sharon Jones

Does this sound familiar? You work with the public every day—customers, clients or patients—and feel so burned out that going to work has become draining. It's always the same questions, problems or complaints. They don't ask for help until it's too late. They won't take time to read or listen to information that you carefully prepared. They ask for advice or guidance and don't take it. If you go out of your way for some people, they don't seem to appreciate it. You start to grit your teeth. Aspects of your job you used to enjoy now seem tedious or less meaningful, and you wonder how much longer you can last.

At one time you were passionate about your career. You spent years acquiring the education and experience to get to this point. And all modesty aside, you are probably highly regarded by peers for your expertise. It seems a little late for a career change. What should you do?

Think for a moment about changing one aspect of your work. Maybe it's the type of people you serve, industry, location or work group.

A college career counselor at a major university applied this strategy. The result was a breakthrough which led to greater intellectual stimulation, renewed energy, increased breadth and depth of knowledge and greater potential for self-employment. What did she do? After working for more than a decade with undergraduate college students in the same major, she felt less empathy for them and stuck at a career plateau.

She ticked off possible risks or losses that could accompany a career or job change:

❂ More than a decade of service toward retirement benefits with her employer

❂ Hard-won national visibility through publishing and public speaking in her field

❂ Potential age discrimination if she applied for new jobs

❂ A husband who was satisfied with his job and worried about potential relocation

Finally the decision was made for her, as she developed health problems: migraines, panic attacks and high blood pressure. She seized an opportunity that seemed less than ideal. A friend, who had relocated twice since they met, called her to talk about a small consulting firm. Independent contractors worked from home to provide career assistance for "trailing spouses" of employees transferred by their corporations. This part-time job from home turned out to be a perfect opportunity to work with a different population—all ages, occupations and industries. She had time in a less stressful environment to recover from her health problems. The job soon became full-time and she was promoted to supervisor, coaching other career counselors working remotely in several states.

After several years, she returned to her previous employer in a different position with the benefit of a much broader background to use in helping students. She was energized and felt the same excitement that she had earlier in her career. Again she became known as an innovator in her profession. As an extra benefit, she knew her background would be valuable in opening a private practice in the future as she eased into retirement.

Becoming a Pioneer

With many occupations experiencing rapid change, you could be on the leading edge, and at the same time overcome burnout with a shift in your specialty. A radiology technician started getting bored after five years on the job. She observed that a little known field in her hospital was rapidly expanding—diagnosis and treatment of sleep disorders. It was new enough that there was a shortage of qualified applicants. In fact, very few colleges even offered a degree in it yet.

She asked her supervisor whether on-the-job training was possible to prepare her for this health field with high demand. This worked out well. She received free training, obtained her certification and is now one of the most experienced sleep technicians in her department.

When she and her husband start a family, this career will offer benefits not available in some other allied health occupations. Many sleep technicians work at night, and her husband could watch their children while she works evenings or weekends.

People are fascinated when they discover what she does for a living, and they ask all kinds of questions. It's exciting being a pioneer in an emerging field. So read about trends in your field, and be ready to watch breakthroughs firsthand!

If you experience continued signs of burnout in your chosen field, try a small shift in your work. You may be able to reinvent yourself by acquiring new skills, meeting fresh challenges and rekindling the spark of passion in your career!

The Power of Magnetic Attraction

By Bev Sincavage, Ph.D.

Sometimes you can get stuck and lose sight of your goals and desires. Just making it through a typical week can overwhelm the larger vision for yourself mapped out at a time when your intentions were strong and your life less chaotic.

What better way to reinforce all your positive desires than to keep them in full view? Feng Shui, the ancient art of placement, uses a map called the Bagua to place reminders of goals throughout your home to bring them into reality. In Feng Shui, every part of your home or any building has significance and meaning, and when these areas are enhanced by placing reminders of your intentions, change occurs. Since your subconscious is always scanning the environment for signals to determine safety or peril, the Bagua uses that innate radar to reinforce desires and good wishes.

Here's a creative solution to make those principles work for you.

How often do you pass your refrigerator door? I would venture several times in a 24-hour period. What a great place to keep your life goals ever present and nudge you to keep moving toward them. Your tool: the **Fridge Bagua**, a smaller version of that map visible to you on a frequent basis. (Or if you prefer, you can create the map on a bulletin board or anywhere you'll see it daily.)

There are nine sections to this grid, representing important areas of your life. The chart below shows how they relate to one another.

The Bagua Grid

Prosperity Color: Purple	**Fame & Reputation** Color: Red	**Relationships** Color: Pink
Family Color: Green	**Health** Color: Yellow	**Creativity & Children** Color: White
Self-Knowledge & Spirituality Color: Blue	**Career** Color: Black	**Helpful People & Travel** Color: Grey

Since each area is also assigned a color, you can use that clue to help you pick out a magnet, or even a photo, to place in each section. Even though these colors are traditionally paired with certain areas of the grid, use only those that feel good to you. Not much of the color is actually needed, maybe only a line or literally a drop.

Let's begin with the first row. The upper left hand corner represents Prosperity. This area governs money and finances but also abundance in any form, including feeling rich with blessings and having a sense of happiness and well-being. Put images of desired objects here or whatever will make you feel "rich" on any level. The middle section, Fame and Reputation, applies to how you are viewed by the outside world as well as your self-esteem and confidence. How do you want to be known? You may want to be known for a particular profession or a specific trait. Gentleness is often represented by a deer, for example. Relationships, found in the upper right hand corner, applies to both love and marriage and your ability to have a loving relationship with yourself. Traditionally, if your are looking to attract or improve a relationship, remember to represent a twosome—two doves, a couple, two of anything.

The middle row includes Family in the left block, Health in the middle and Creativity and Children in the right block. Family is represented by both your close friends, blood relatives and ancestors. You could add a quote or affirmation that pertains to an ideal family or to your close circle of friends. Moving to the middle section, we encounter Health. This section represents your personal physical health. To ensure your health stays high or to give it a boost, be sure whatever you put here is vibrant and ideal, like flowers. In Creativity and

Children, all aspects of creativity are represented, including arts and crafts and the ultimate creation, children. Depending on your intention, you can be as creative and whimsical as you wish.

The last row begins with Self-Knowledge and Spirituality. As you can see, it spans both the knowledge we gain from learning and scholarship, and the inner knowledge of spiritual wisdom. Affirmations can be added to this area or items that represent spirituality to you. Placing a library magnet here would represent all the knowledge you have acquired and your continued quest for learning. The middle section, Career, deals with how you earn your living or how you want to. If you would like to change careers, represent your new job here. If you are happy with what you are doing, represent that feeling with a symbol that expresses the positive facets of your career. (Note that the Career section deals with how you actually make a living, while Fame represents how you wish to be seen by the outside world. Sometimes they are the same, but often they have different goals.) The last area in the lower right hand corner is Helpful People and Travel. In addition to travel, the helpful people aspect includes all the people you encounter: mentors, clients, colleagues, even the plumber. A "smiley face" magnet would be perfect here.

The goal of the Fridge Bagua is to keep those aspects of your life that are working well in balance and to nourish those areas that you want to change. Simply by glancing at your magnet/photo map, your mind remembers your greater vision and appreciates your current gifts and accomplishments.

To construct the Bagua, mentally imagine the grid on your refrigerator door and then fill in the spaces with anything you think appropriate for that section. Really have fun with this project and be as creative as you like by searching for interesting and representative magnets, then simply arrange them according to the Bagua grid. No one but you has to know what they mean. If you can't find the exact magnet, make your own with a treasured object, a hot glue gun and small magnets available at craft stores.

You get the idea—let your imagination wander. The only requirement is that you really like the magnet or photo and that it represents a positive feeling to you. This is no place for negative thinking!

So have fun and remember that by keeping your goals and desires always in view, you'll bring them into form much sooner.

Break Through, Give In and Grow Up!

By Rhoberta Shaler, Ph.D.

It takes a lot to be a grown-up. Not a looking-like, "pretending to be until something goes wrong" kind of grown-up, but a real one. I raised three children mostly as a single parent and earned three university degrees while working full-time and receiving little child support. You'd think that would make me a grown-up.

I've accepted responsibility, been accountable and lived in integrity. Good grown-up behaviors. I've known and repeated all the right things and I've done well. In the eyes of the world, I have excelled at Grown-up School. Yet, I knew better. Deep in my heart, and in the back of my mind, I knew there was something more. I did not want to feel like an impostor in the rare world of true grown-ups.

As a psychologist, international speaker and author of a bunch of books, I know this stuff. In fact, I usually live by it with some semblance of predictability. So it's not about behaving as a grown-up, as much as it is *feeling* like one.

There's a big difference between doing the behaviors and achieving the results. It's the difference between doing the right thing and having the right reasons. I think of the times I did the right thing for the approval of others, as compared to doing it because it was authentic for my values and who I am. That's just part of growing up. We do often want to please our parents, after all. Grown-ups, though, behave from their values regardless of the audience.

Once I was working with a coaching client in a large organization. He spent the majority of his time trying to figure out what his superiors wanted from him. Should he be like this? Should he react like that? Should he hold back or speak up? All good questions in some contexts. However, he was hired because of his skills, creativity and enthusiasm. Unless he had the confidence to be himself and demonstrate the very things for which he was hired, disappointment all around would be the result. Once he unpacked his fears of disapproval and focused on what he brought to the position, he shined. He was himself—the person they hired.

So what are the criteria for being an authentic grown-up?

It took many years on the planet, much work on myself and several true dark nights of the soul to get a glimpse into what it might mean.

A very wise man in my life reminded me that no matter what anyone else is doing, the choices I make reflect who I am regardless of the people involved, the circumstances or the conditions. When I can answer the question, "Who am I?" in the most complete sense, then I always know how to behave. That's authenticity.

The daily practice of reminding myself that I have a choice about my responses to life—it seems like a hundred times a minute some days—takes great focus, willingness and attention. I have learned that when I slow down and remember who I am, I make better choices. I become much easier to live with internally. I like myself. Integrity feels good. Life flows.

Recently, I undertook a half-time, nine-month contract in another country. It was an unexpected opportunity to rebuild an ailing organization. When I stepped into the role, all eyes—and bets—were on me to turn things around. I did, and quickly. Within two months, attendance at the weekly meetings of the group swelled from 90 to 180. Good return in terms of time and money.

Then things got tough. Board members vied for control, visibility and power. Apparently, the success of the organization was less important to some than their egos. Things became chaotic. Someone asked why I stayed. The answer was simple: I cared about the people and the organization and I had a contract. Honoring it is who I am and what I'm about.

I am thankful for that experience, even though there were some very dark moments. At those times, I had the opportunity to remind myself to behave from what I believed and demonstrate it in every thought, word and action. Emerging from it, my grown-up self knew I had done the right thing for the right reasons at the right time.

And that's where the "giving in" part of the equation surfaces. Surrendering to doing the right thing *for me* was key. Staying true to my values in circumstances that were less than ideal was a prime opportunity for an aspiring grown-up. Not giving up, but giving in to the lesson in the best possible way to extract the maximum value from the experience is where growth occurs.

Surrender has deep spiritual meaning for me. Whether or not that is a compelling value for others, I advocate giving up the need to be in control of every circumstance. I have enough work to do on myself without focusing my time and energy on changing others. It's not about them. It's about me living my values. It's about who I choose to be moment to moment. I must speak and act from my truth. I know there is a bigger action at work in my life, and I live without attachment to my outcomes—on my best days, that is.

It's that simple, but it's often not that easy! And, I've learned, it's certainly not for the faint-hearted. Being a grown-up is a full-time job.

Here are a few things I learned:

❂ **Grown-ups tell the truth.** How many people wait for the right time to say what needs to be said? I'm not suggesting anyone be insensitive, but really now, is there ever a good time? You're doing mental gymnastics trying to make the truth palatable, maybe even acceptable, AND you want good timing? Just tell the truth in the kindest, most honest and respectful way possible.

❂ **Grown-ups handle things as they come up.** When grown-ups are in a relationship, they count on each other to communicate fully. They practice respectful and responsible communication. No exaggeration. No defamation. Just the facts. They listen well, remain curious about the other person and take the time to create agreements. No "hit-and run" behaviors.

❂ **Grown-ups take personal responsibility for their thoughts, feelings and actions.** Tough though it can be, grown-ups are not looking for who caused their past pain, anger, sadness or loss and engaging in a litany of blame. That's a big one. It's easy to stay stuck for a lifetime if your daily chant is: "Ain't it awful," "If only…" and "He done me wrong." Grown-ups give up whining, blaming, sniveling, groveling and making excuses.

❂ **Grown-ups live from their internal truth, no matter what the circumstances or conditions.** The motivation to live joyfully each day comes from the clarity of their values and the alignment of their words and behaviors with those values. They know who they are and act accordingly. They show up, speak up and step up. They live to express their authentic selves, not for the approval of others.

Life is filled with lessons. A good friend gave me a small embroidered pillow that never fails to bring a smile to my face as it reminds me what to do. It reads, "*Put on your big girl panties and deal with it.*" That's good advice.

Good students break through, give in and grow up. They graduate from Grown-Up School summa cum laude. And for me, the clarity, peace and joy is worth the work.

Every Problem Has Many Solutions

By Nancy Grant

A classic way you can get stuck in your life is by convincing yourself you have no options but to remain where you are. But that is just never true. This stuck point is easiest to tackle with input from others who *can* see beyond your mindset. You can always ask for help, and for some of you, that in itself is a challenge.

Start by making a list of everyone you know who you'd consider talking to about your issue. Then write down people you know of but don't know personally, who might be able to help. Now add those up and multiply by ten—or if you're stubbornly pessimistic—by five. That number represents the additional people who might help, who are known to the people on your own list. That number should give you some encouragement. Surely *someone* from that list will have some ideas for you!

Next, start asking for help, even though it may make you feel vulnerable. And *always* ask everyone you speak to for *other* people you might consult. The results may surprise you, especially if you aren't used to doing this. Many, many people are willing to be of service to others—often because they've seen their good efforts return to them or they've been on the receiving end themselves.

Almost every kind of professional person may offer a free initial consultation. That's a tremendous no-cost resource right there. And if they can't help, remember to ask for referrals. It's all about networking.

And speaking of that, if you don't already, try attending some local professional meetings related to your business, such as a chamber of commerce, Soroptimist or trade association meeting. Those occasions are built for the purpose of networking and connecting people. If your challenge is of a more personal nature, look for relevant support groups. Many newspapers publish lists of such meetings, or search online.

Another tactic is to request informational interviews from professionals whose brains you want to pick. This is especially useful if you are considering a job or career change. Or perhaps you're thinking of moving to a new area—don't be afraid to ask people you see in stores or parks about the quality of life in their neighborhood. Never underestimate the kindness of strangers!

The real point of this tactic is to remember that you don't have to solve your problem alone. Help is always just a phone call or email away.

A Better Business Decision: Problem-Solving the Shamanic Way

By Jacke Schroeder

We all reach points in our business decision making process where we have several crucial paths we can take. Will it be worth the time and effort to start a particular business venture? Who should we hire, and will they help or hurt the business? Should we expand or stay put for the time being? These decisions are essential, but also confounding. It can be difficult to feel certain we're making the right choices, and sometimes we just end up making important decisions by default. We examine all the facts, and we do what seems best in light of the information we have.

The word *information* is key, because the information we have about any situation is very limited by our perceptions, our personal inclinations, and known factors such as finances, qualifications, goals and ideals. Access to information beyond what we currently know would improve our ability to make good choices.

To help business owners choose which path to pursue, I use Shamanism, a practice available to all, to access a deeper level of information. In addition, it empowers business owners and employees with a connection to their own spiritual guides. This has proved to be very successful in everything from discovering solutions for known business problems to restructuring and organizational decisions.

So what is Shamanism, and how is it proving extremely useful in this day and age?

Shamanism is a way of perceiving the nature of the universe. It's an ancient way of seeing, hearing, feeling, knowing, understanding and experiencing communications beyond what is known in ordinary reality.

Throughout history, Shamanism has been practiced on every continent in the world. A shaman or shamanic practitioner is one who "sees" in the dark, aided by repetitive and monotonous sound that comes from drum beats or rattles, which changes brain waves inducing an alpha or theta state—facilitating a shift in consciousness.

This shift enables the practitioner to connect with her spirit helpers, the ones responsible for the healing, guidance and practical information. Journeying is the practice that is the pathway to those spirit helpers for the shamanic practitioner, who becomes the conduit through which the healing and guiding messages are transmitted.

Since businesses are filled with spirit, and since shamanism works with the spiritual aspect of illness, when businesses are struggling or are "sick," it follows that shamanism is a natural method for bringing healing. Your business is not just a business, but an entity made up of people and spirit connected to all of life.

When there is a disconnect between your business and its spirit, that sometimes results in low staff morale and productivity, burn-out, inefficiency, blocked creativity, trouble meeting goals and deadlines, cash flow problems, decrease in sales, general misfortune and many other problems.

The goal of Shamanism as applied to businesses is the reunion with lost spiritual power. Journeying and meeting with spirit allies enriches and empowers businesses and the lives of people working for them. In addition to empowerment, shamanic practices for business are aimed at assessment, planning, outcomes evaluation, staffing, team building, mediation and mergers.

For example, the owner of an accounting firm who wanted guidance in making a new hire called me for help. The candidate had tested positively in the psychological evaluations, particularly in loyalty. But some people at the firm were concerned that he didn't have longevity in his work history—to the point that the owner wanted to, but felt uncomfortable with hiring him, but she couldn't put her finger on what was bothering her.

To help her make the choice, I journeyed for what her firm might encounter if she did, in fact, hire him. The information I came up with was that he was extremely loyal, as the test had indicated—but to his family, not to work. Therefore, his responsibilities would go unattended because he would be absent too often. I relayed this information to the business owner. Not long after that, the potential employee told the owner his wife was ill.

On another occasion, I was called to Arizona to facilitate a meeting aimed at the merger between an IT business and a research and evaluation consulting firm. I taught the potential partners to journey for their power animals. While sharing information from their journeys, it became evident to them both that their personalities were not suited to a partnership with one another. They were so grateful not to have spent a lot of time and money discovering they weren't a good business match—one which most likely would have resulted in a painful and failed venture.

The practice of Shamanism is harmless, kind, compassionate, fun and joyful—although the recognition of ethical behavior is imperative when journeying about the impact of others on your business. Be sure that the intent is for the betterment of the business, not simply to investigate another person without their permission.

Some examples of questions to inspire divination journeys:

❂ How can I heal my business?

❂ Where should I look for a home for my business?

❂ What will my business encounter if I hire John Doe?

❂ What will my experience be if I hire John Doe?

❂ What will I learn if I make this choice?

❂ What do I need to do to offer the best product or service?

❂ How can I heal my relationship with my CEO?

❂ What changes do I need to make in my business to increase revenue?

- What are some simple practices my staff can use throughout the day to improve morale?
- What is the power ally or animal of my business or organization?
- How can my power animal help me restore balance and harmony in the work environment?
- What are the next three steps to take to realize a successful business merger?

The utilization of this practice is gaining momentum, with several thousand practitioners across the United States. For more information, you can contact me to learn to journey, even by telephone. Or you can visit www.shamanism.org (the Foundation for Shamanic Studies) to find a practitioner in your area. Or to read a fable written by Richard Whiteley about shamanism being applied in a business, check out www.corpshaman.com. Finally, online searches for Shamanism will produce a bounty of resources.

Achievable, Sustainable Outcomes

By Morgan McCartor

The path from underearning to stretching to become all that we can be is composed of a series of smaller outcomes that build on each other. The result can be an outcome that might have seemed, in the beginning, breathtaking.

Many outcomes, however, cannot be sustained. One way to meet this challenge is to use *framing* to focus on what is important, and *reframing* to address certain issues that get in the way of progress.

People often get stuck in a pattern of cycling that makes sustaining an outcome impossible. We become dissatisfied with where we are, and decide to stretch for more. However, going outside the comfort zone leads to other discomforts.

In stretching from the old unsatisfactory state to our new desired outcome:

❂ We may leave behind things we value, such as the comfort of always knowing what to do, old friendships or a comfortable salary.

❂ We may encounter things we don't want, such as frustration when things we try don't pan out, fear of the unknown or conflict with family beliefs.

We are inherently drawn toward comfort and away from discomfort. If we act out of seeking to restore comfort, we end up cycling between the desired outcome and the old state. Discomfort associated with the new sends us back toward the old, and dissatisfaction with the old sends us forward toward the new. We cycle instead of progressing.

For example, you might decide to become more organized, but as you accomplish it, begin to feel rebellion against bowing to others' demands. You may stop making the effort. As you become less organized again, the problems of being disorganized—lost time, late bills, feelings of guilt—will take their toll, sending you back in the direction of being organized.

Notice your own cycles. You might want to write them down.

There is a way to end the cycling. Robert Fritz, who has dedicated years studying how individuals and organizations create or fail to create outcomes, points out that cycling occurs because we give the same weight to the desired outcome and to the old state. We can end the cycling by giving the desired outcome precedence. Then the outcome becomes the frame of reference for all decisions about what to do, and issues become things that must be addressed.

For example, if being organized is your desired outcome, the discomfort of feeling rebellious becomes an issue to be addressed, not something to be given into.

Start with assuring that your outcome is well-formed, which means the outcome has the possibility of being both attained and sustained.

The following list is based on the criteria for a well-formed outcome, developed in the neuro-linguistic programming community:

❂ The outcome must be stated in positive terms. Aim toward what you want, not away from what you don't want. For example, saying: "I want a different job" is negative. All it says is that you want to go away from where you are. Any direction will do, and you could get something less desirable. Instead, saying: "I want work that uses my talent of communicating and will pay me twice as much as I'm now earning" aims at something you want. **Ask yourself: What do I want?** Be detailed in your answer.

❂ The outcome must connect with your passion or internal drive. External motivation or trying to motivate yourself will not do. You need that inner fire to sustain you when challenges arise. **Ask yourself: What will I get by having this outcome? And what is important about that?**

❂ Progress must be measurable. Some of what you do will be trial and error, and you must be able to tell if your efforts result in progress. **Ask yourself: How will I know when I get my outcome?**

❂ You must have the necessary resources. However, remember that the imagination—yours or others'—can be magical in defining and finding new or unexpected resources. **Ask yourself: What resources do I need?**

❂ Positive things left behind and negative things encountered must be addressed. Approaches to addressing these issues are discussed below. However, it is possible for an issue to be such that it can't be addressed. Then the outcome needs adjusting. For example, a given outcome may require too big a stretch for now. Or maybe the consequences of failure are too great. **Ask yourself: What will I lose by having this outcome? What will I gain that I don't want?**

❂ Make any adjustments needed to make your outcome well-formed. Using the outcome as your frame of reference will give you focus. **Ask: Given what I want to achieve, what is the best thing to do next? Does what I'm doing serve my outcome?**

Give the outcome precedence, then address discomfort issues as they arise. There are two ways to address an issue: change the issue itself, or leave the issue alone, but change its significance. For example, if you experience anxiety at lacking a skill needed in your new job, you can change the circumstance directly by developing the skill or by collaborating with someone else.

However, if you are subjected to discrimination, you may not be able to address the issue directly. What you can do is to change the significance of the discrimination. If the discrimination is really upsetting, reframe it as something that makes you feel a bit peevish (a silly-sounding word that can bleed away fervor). Or reframe it as signifying that you are a pioneer and need to build bridges. Or reframe it as indicating that you are perceived as a powerful contender who needs containment, and savor it. The substance of the issue won't change, but when its meaning does, so will your response. Choose a reframe that supports your outcome.

Here are some tips for dealing with these particular challenges.

❂ **Fear:** In any frame in which you are going beyond your comfort zone, you need an expanded understanding of what fear indicates and how to respond to it. Fear could conceivably still signal the need to prepare to fight or run. More likely, it signals unfamiliar territory and the need to be attentive. Or the feeling might be an indicator of appropriate stretching, as required by the outcome. Then the most appropriate response might be gratitude. Or the sensation might be meaningless, and the best response simply to feel the feeling.

❂ **Frustration:** Frustration is a sensation often interpreted as indicating that something ought to be different. In the frame of creating an outcome, frustration signals the need to change either your actions or your expectations. For example, becoming a consultant usually takes several years. Frustration at having few clients after a year might mean a need to change expectations. After three years, it might indicate a need to change tactics in developing clients.

❂ **Resistance to being organized:** People have all sorts of considerations about becoming organized—issues of style, power and the time involved. In the context of achieving outcomes, the purpose of organization is to be ready for action, especially for taking advantage of unexpected opportunities. What constitutes being organized depends upon the needs of the person and the situation.

❂ **Confusion:** Confusion is often interpreted as indicating that something is wrong. However, when acting outside the comfort zone, confusion could be a simple signal for the need to acquire more information, or it could indicate that old thought patterns and beliefs are breaking up, and new, more useful ones have not yet replaced them. Confusion could be welcomed as an indication of growth.

Outcomes are the bricks that form the path forward, so it is to our advantage to become skilled at the art of achieving and sustaining them. The criteria for a well-formed outcome, Fritz's approach of giving precedence to the outcome and the use of reframing to address issues are three good starts.

Helping Others To Help Yourself

By Ginger Hilley

Being a widow was new to me. I felt alone and isolated. Yet I eventually arrived at a place where I was ready to move forward with my life, but fear and confusion kept me immobilized. I didn't know how to make forward strides. I had the desire but not the know-how to begin rebuilding my shattered life.

Then one day I just decided no one could do this for me. That meant only one thing. I would have to do it for and by myself. But how? Where should I begin?

Community service seemed like a logical place to start. After all, what did I really have to loose? They couldn't fire me if I messed up, and I wouldn't have the same type of demands placed upon me as if I was getting paid for my efforts.

I began to explore the next step of this journey and figure out where I would spend my time. Previously, I had been involved with crisis phone lines and had also spent a considerable amount of time volunteering with children in various organizations. Given the circumstances, I didn't feel either was a good option for me at that time.

A logical place for my involvement finally presented itself in the form of a therapeutic home for young girls that needed some additional resources. That is where I chose to begin moving forward again. It was great! I spent about a year with them, mentoring and leading some basic life skills classes. Slowly, things began to shift for me, and I sought out different experiences.

Discovering what I wanted to do gradually evolved by narrowing it down from what I *didn't* want to do. It was a process of elimination. This part is important when you step out to devote your time and energy to serving others. It's important to have a level of integrity during your involvement, and the best way I know to do that is by being committed, on whatever level, to your service to others.

You receive something intangible when you commit to serving others. Many people I know give with ulterior motives. And to be honest, I have to say on some level this is also what I did. I gave of my time and energy in order to feel better, but I also knew this was a vehicle for change within myself.

This is an integral part of becoming unstuck and moving your life forward in a positive manner. It is really more about the perspective you hold onto about your situation. The byproduct of devoting some enthusiasm to a cause other than yourself, is that you are rewarded through vicarious participation.

I suggest that people not have a preconceived idea of what the experience of getting unstuck should look or feel like. The Nike mantra of "Just do it!" applies to taking that first step out the door. Remember, baby steps. You don't have to set out to change the world. It might be something as simple as offering to pick up groceries for an ill neighbor or walking their dog. It's the simple things that are often most powerful.

Consider community service. It can validate the very purpose of our lives and help to get us going. The cause to which we devote our time is less important than the action itself. It turned out to be the best thing I could possibly have done. Volunteering got me to begin the networking process that I had put on hold. I picked general causes that interested me on some level. Some causes I have stayed with, and many I have moved beyond, but the benefit of each interaction was invaluable. By giving to others, I truly received innumerable gifts in return.

Today, I work with many people in grief recovery and with people in careers that are dissatisfying. One thing I always encourage these people to do, is pick a cause they can relate to and volunteer. A big time commitment is not necessary, nor is it always appropriate. Four hours per month is enough. It's a great way to create movement in your life.

Mental Roadblocks

By Elizabeth M. Johnson

For many women, one of the roadblocks to success is purely mental. Unconsciously, they somehow become stuck. Rendered immobile by self-doubt, fear, guilt, images of perfection, societal expectations and other inner obstacles, women permit these roadblocks to hold them back from success. However, these roadblocks are entirely mental ones, so they are within our locus of control.

Mental roadblocks are often by-products of low self-esteem. Imagine a current roadblock in your own life. Got one? Okay, now think about what's stopping you from getting beyond it. At the very heart of the roadblock, is there an issue that relates to self-esteem? Consider these common roadblocks: not making enough money; a relationship lacking tenderness; insufficient time for self; anxiety over making a career change. If these scenarios sound familiar, then you're like 85% of the women who come to me, women whose low self-esteem in one area or another has created roadblocks in their lives that halt their personal and professional success.

The way to leap over roadblocks and keep them behind you is to follow the path of the Authentic Self. You *could* practice the Band-Aid approach, which eliminates the roadblock by simply avoiding it, choosing to not address the real issue at hand. This approach, however, does not prevent future roadblocks, because nothing has truly been dealt with. The Authentic Self is who you *really* are, the inner person at the core of your being.

When you follow the path of your Authentic Self, your self-esteem increases. With increased self-esteem, you gain greater confidence in your abilities. You accept that you have the right to satisfaction and success, and you discover your personal power grows exponentially, enabling you to deal more effectively with any of the challenges (formerly roadblocks) that life throws your way.

The Authentic Self path is an effective way to transform mental roadblocks from stopping points into personal growth opportunities.

The following are four ways to build self-esteem and live the Authentic Self to effectively combat those nasty roadblocks:

1. Resist the temptation to strive for perfection. The tendency toward perfection can sneak into any life as quickly as a greyhound out of the gate. *Perfect* is anti-authentic, however. When you attempt to introduce perfection into something, the Authentic Self ceases to exist. Perfection is an unattainable ideal that has a parasitic existence—it thrives by perpetuating self-doubt. Conversely, authenticity by its very nature nourishes the self by embracing personal uniqueness, which diminishes any inner angst. Personal growth stops with perfection, but it dances and thrives with authenticity. My clients learn to celebrate their authenticity by reminding themselves that different is good. Remember that attempting perfection is a choice. You can choose to strive for perfection in your life and struggle with the barrage of roadblocks that come your way, *or* you can choose authenticity and embrace the clarity of perspective that comes when you're following your own true path.

2. Notice the shoulds. *Should* and its evil twin *must* steer you away from your Authentic Self. They are danger words fattened with weighty emotions like guilt and fear. When you use *should* and *must*, you shrink your self-esteem, and the roadblocks that hinder your success begin to multiply. Don't let it happen. If a *should* sneaks into one of your sentences or thoughts, promptly kick its butt right out the front door and watch the guilt and fear diminish. When you use *should* as a way to measure your life, you can count on consistently coming up short and being vexed at every turn you make. Just ask: By whose standard are you measuring yourself when you use *should*? Certainly not the standard of your Authentic Self.

3. Re-appreciate your passions and wishes. Passions and wishes are energy sources. They feed your Authentic Self. When you acknowledge them and do some dreaming about what it takes to bring them to fruition, you start the process of actualizing them. This actualization nourishes your Authentic Self. Because passions and wishes are part of your Authentic Self, they are valid and real. Acknowledge them for the powerful source they are, not as a whim or nonsensical idea that is better off unspoken. When you accept the power that passions and wishes hold, your Authentic Self emerges and self-esteem grows. With passions and wishes as the pulse of our actions, roadblocks cease to become lifeless dead ends and become possibility-filled passageways instead.

4. Enlist a support team. Identify a few members of your own support team—folks who are there to champion you. Having a support team will remind you that you are not alone in the world. Sometimes when we feel stuck, the simple voice of a friend gives us the strength and encouragement to keep going. A support team will also help you offset and minimize any failures, while simultaneously championing your Authentic Self. I recommend a support team outside the family. Family members are generally too emotionally tied to us. They often cannot champion your success or share your challenges without translating your words into actions that affect them. And don't forget to ask for what you need from your support team. The act of accessing your support team for what you need will do wonders in knocking down roadblocks to success.

Roadblocks are a fact of life. But they needn't become a stuck place where you languish waiting for someone to hear your SOS. Instead of waiting for someone to save the situation or save you, readjust your thinking instead. When you switch to an Authentic Self mindset, the possibilities for success become more easily visible through the lens of increased self-esteem. Women who live their Authentic Selves are eye-catching cool, not cookie-cutter same. It becomes exciting to look around, below, above, through and beyond that roadblock which had initially seemed daunting. Allow your Authentic Self to guide your actions, and you will find your life is filled with satisfaction, personal integrity and meaningful success.

Living A Thankful Life

by Rev. Christine Green

Did you know the brain does not know the difference between what is imagined and what is real? When we focus on the challenges facing us, we begin to worry. When we worry we begin to spin a tale of *What ifs*. The mind fantasizes about what might happen. The brain doesn't know that we're just imagining it, so it triggers negative emotions, which cause stress in the body that results in fear. Fear then causes us to look around and see even more things that are not working. Suddenly we seem to be frozen in time, unable to move.

A great way to change your emotional energy and lift your spirit is an act of gratitude. University of California psychologist, Robert Emmons, reports that gratitude exercises improve physical health, raise energy levels and can even relieve pain and fatigue for patients with neuromuscular disease.

Some years ago, I found myself in a frustrating job with nowhere to go. I heard about an opening with a company that was exactly what I was looking for. I eagerly applied for the new job and was asked back on three interviews. I was sure it was mine. Instead, I received the devastating call, "Sorry, we gave the job to someone with more experience." I was stunned. I was already mentally moving out of my cubicle…now I was stuck there.

After a period of feeling sorry for myself, I knew it was up to me to see things differently. I changed my focus from grieving about what I didn't have, to giving thanks for what I did have. I started feeling grateful that I *had* a job. It was small place to start. Then I noticed how supportive my supervisor was, and the fact that she let me have flexible time for doctor appointments. A new computer was delivered from a request I had made two months earlier.

As my attitude changed, it felt like things around me also changed. I was given a project to work on that I really wanted. Just about the time I was thinking I could actually *like* that job, my supervisor approached me about an opening in another department that would be a promotion. Long story short...I applied and the promotion was mine.

Universal Law states: Whatever we are grateful for increases. You can stop the flow of negative energy by shifting your focus. Try taking your attention off the problem and redirect it toward something you are grateful for.

Here are three steps that may be helpful in gratitude building when you are in the midst of strife.

❂ First, take a deep breath and release the energy you are holding. Breathing is essential for life and is so often taken for granted. Visualize breathing in as receiving and breathing out as releasing. The breath is an important link between your body, mind and spirit.

❂ Second, step back and observe your situation. Find the things you can appreciate, regardless how insignificant they may seem. Make a list of everything that is working in your life. Writing them all down makes them real.

❂ Third, call, write or email at least one person and confide why you are grateful for them.

The practice of gratitude begins to lift us out of the emotion of the situation. As our emotions change, so does our experience.

We are so blessed as women to be living in a country where we have freedom and opportunities to express ourselves and follow our dreams. I invite you to engage that freedom and make living a thankful life part of your expression. Enjoy the results!

SCRAM: How To Move Through and Move Beyond Your Stuck State

By Nancy D. Solomon

Sit still
Change your focus
Remember who you are
Ask the important questions
Move forward one step at a time

People get stuck for a reason—we just don't always know what that reason is. Then we get so hung up on being stuck that we become even more stuck. And so the cycle perpetuates itself. What I've discovered from coaching and counseling hundreds of people just like you and me, is that there is a wealth of wisdom imbued in every moment we are stuck. Perhaps we're stuck simply because we're moving too fast, we're off purpose or our lives are leading us instead of the other way around.

How do you change all that, you ask? How do you shine like a stadium light when you feel like a refrigerator bulb? How do you get unstuck? Well, you SCRAM, of course. I've used SCRAM for the past twenty years—it's a way to get back on track when it looks like the car you're supposed to be driving is moving on without you.

In the beginning of your journey back to yourself, it's important to follow these steps in the prescribed sequence. Once you've begun to listen to your inner wisdom, trust yourself and follow your own unique and divine path, then hop around as you please.

Here's how SCRAM works:

❂ **Sit still.** I've worked with so many people who have gotten stuck just so that they have an excuse to stand still. We live in a culture that richly rewards action junkies. We rally to do more and more, and we receive accolades for exhausting ourselves. We work harder and faster at the things that don't work rather than stop, stand still and examine the overall workability of our lives. If you're willing to consciously press the pause button on your life, sit still and access the intuitive voice within you, then often you'll receive guidance and peace that will direct you to a more purposeful (and unstuck) place.

❂ **Choose your focus.** Our society is pathology-centered, emphasizing the things that need to be fixed, changed or obliterated from existence. I'd suggest that focusing on our weaknesses is like pumping up the flat side of a tire. (For the car-repair impaired, pumping up the flat side of a tire is impossible, it doesn't get you anywhere and it is an absolute waste of time.) I find it much more useful to steer my clients toward their strengths. Your gifts and talents and the things that are most natural, easy and enjoyable will inevitably help you to discover what's right with you, thereby changing the entire focus of your life.

❂ **Remember who you are.** Competition can be lethal medicine—it can destroy your creativity and talent on contact. When you walk your own path without looking at the other side of the street, when you live from the inside out, you are happiest and most joyful because you're on purpose and fulfilling your destiny. Frequently we get stuck because we're imitating life instead of living it—we're living someone else's lie about us. I'd strongly urge you to have at least one person in your life who will remind you of who you are when you forget.

❂ **Ask the important questions.** The simplest way to become unstuck is to ask yourself the really difficult questions—the ones you absolutely, positively do *not* want to know the answers to! Inherent in every question lies the answer. Questioning evokes change. There is a tendency to ask yourself about the concrete and physical results you want when, paradoxically, the universal currency is emotion and spirit. The latter is counter-intuitive to our culture. For instance, people who are stuck in a job they don't like will normally ask themselves: "What job do I want to do?" or "What's the next logical move I should make?" or "I wonder if I should change careers?" Those types of questions, however, will often generate a different form of the same hell. It is far more productive to ask yourself how you want to feel in that new position, or what emotional experience you want to achieve. When you focus on the feeling, the opportunities seem to be more abundant and fulfilling.

❂ **Move forward one step at a time.** Take a step—it doesn't even matter which one or how teeny it is—movement begets movement. Growth of any sort begins with the willingness to do so.

When you find the courage to do one little thing differently, to look forward instead of wallow in your issue, it sends a gigantic message to the universe—it says you're ready to put some energy behind the resolution of this concern. Small steps also send a message back to you that you're ready to break the pattern of being stuck. You have control over one enormous thing in your life, and that one enormous thing is midway between your two ears. Yup, it's your mind and it's your attitude.

Lastly, I would remind you of three things. First, when you're in the shadow of inertia, when it seems impossible to move a millimeter, it's very useful to remember that you have been stuck before, and at some point, you became unstuck. It's very rare to find someone who has remained stuck indefinitely.

Next, is the reminder that you are not the problem you have. When you say, "I'm stuck," it makes you the problem, when it's more likely external forces that thwart your movement. Outside opinion or expectation causes us to judge and second-guess ourselves, both of which compel us to put the brakes on in order to question our reality.

Finally, I truly believe we need to give ourselves permission to be stuck to begin with. The only thing wrong with being stuck is that, well, we *think* it's wrong! What if, instead, we celebrated being stuck, because our internal alarm alerted us to the fact that things are off kilter, and being stuck gives us an opportunity to make things right? I'd venture to say that if we reframed stuck it wouldn't stick as long as it does.

Three Radical Moves for Living Unstuck

By Inga Estes

At one time or another most of us have felt stuck, trapped somewhere between where we started and where we're headed. For some people this sense of being stuck is temporary, while for others it has seemingly become a way of life. But what if it was impossible to actually get stuck?

Think of it: nothing in our universe is stuck. Planets spin, water evaporates, ice melts, oceans have tides, seeds sprout into plants, seasons change and even mountains erupt and transform themselves. If Nature herself is showing us that everything is always in a state of flow, what does this imply for us personally? Is it only because we have labeled ourselves as being stuck that this has become true for us?

We say "I'm stuck" to describe a situation in our lives when we feel stagnant—helpless, hopeless or uncertain of our ability to shape our own future. We often believe that we have tried to no avail and become resigned to the Realm of Stuck, blind to other options or choices. However, as we learn from the world around us, everything is in motion. Could it be that we're not seeing progress, or we're not seeing it happen fast enough, and we're just calling ourselves stuck? Many times we aren't even aware of the consequences of declaring: "I'm stuck."

Believing or saying "I'm stuck" is self-limiting. Saying that is like putting ourselves into a tiny little room and turning off the lights. From that perspective, we see and feel only the dark, the fear and the hopelessness of having no options. We become immobilized.

And yet it is only because we have labeled ourselves as stuck that we have become constricted. We seem to settle in and stop looking for options; we are now in a defensive, survival mode. Once we say "I'm stuck" we become less likely to take the risks necessary to meet our goals, and more importantly, when we feel stuck we also become less and less aware that we have the ability at any moment to turn on the lights and walk out of our dark little room.

So what does it take to turn on the lights?

It's this simple: When you feel stuck, the first thing to ask yourself is, "What am I paying attention to—am I focusing too much on how stuck I feel, rather than paying attention to what I want to accomplish?" Are you generating a confining conversation, one that keeps you locked up in a small dark room? Or, instead, could you generate a bigger and richer conversation which allows you to build confidence and a greater sense of creating your own future?

One of the greatest tools for living the life of an optimist is to realize that in any given moment we have choices regarding our thinking and our language. With respect to feeling stuck then, let's first realize we have created this interpretation, and we have only ourselves to thank for putting us into that dark little room. In the moment we acknowledge our responsibility for doing that, we begin to have some choices.

In that exact nano-second when we realize we have defined our situation as stuck, we can also choose to say something new that expands rather than contracts our options. We can say, "Hmm…things are not going as I imagined, and I'm staying open to new ideas, new input and new practices."

We can also ask a friend or colleague to collaborate with us about this and help us brainstorm. We can ask: "What am I not seeing?"

When we create this attitude of openness and inquiry, our frustration begins to ease and we quickly feel the movement come back into our lives. We're back to being in the natural flow of the universe, and from there, can often see new choices and options that we just couldn't see a little while earlier.

Here are three radical moves to help you stay in the flow and expand your ability to move through fear, immobilization and feelings of inadequacy that arise when you define yourself as being stuck.

***Radical Move #1:* Eliminate stuck thinking and speaking.**

Starting right now, how about obliterating the idea that getting stuck is even possible? What would happen if you committed to eliminating that idea and phrase from your vocabulary? And be easy on yourself when you find yourself back in the quagmire of stuckness—it's a habit that will take patience, practice and persistence to overcome. And learn from your lapses—it's not about never feeling stuck again—it's about noticing and catching yourself earlier every time the bad habit wants to return.

***Radical Move #2:* Fill the void.**

Rather than focusing on what's missing, pay attention to what you want to create. Where do you want to end up? Always keep sight of your intention and your desired result, rather than allowing obstacles and barriers to distract you, block your view and keep you from your destination. It is this clarity that gives you the juice to create and fulfill your dreams.

***Radical Move #3:* Socialize your new thinking.**

Empathy is important, but you don't want to accidentally reinforce what you're trying to eliminate. So don't whine or complain about how stuck you are, and don't let your friends commiserate with you. Instead, create a conspiracy of intention that redirects your attention. Get into cahoots with friends and colleagues about what it is that each of you wants to achieve and how to better support each other. That way, your conspiracy is to lift each other up, not drag each other down into misery.

Use these three radical moves so when you, your friends, family or colleagues see each other locked in one of those dark little rooms, you can knock on the door or bang on the wall to remind each other that there is a light switch and a door! "*Hey, over there, on your right—yeah, that's it, a little farther—yup, keep going!*"

Contributors

Current contact information for the contributors, including web and email addresses, can be found at: www.BreakingThroughBook.com

Katana Abbott, CFP
Smart Women's Coaching
Commerce, MI
With 20 years experience as a financial planner, Katana is uniquely qualified to help women reinvent their lives with purpose, passion and prosperity. Visit her website to take advantage of her free seven-part digital audio mini course "The Perfect Life Focus" and sign up for her "Smart Women, Smart Choices," newsletter, workshops, coaching and retreats.
www.smartwomenscoaching.com

Allison Acken, Ph.D.
Womentalkmoney.com
Los Angeles, CA
Allison is a clinical psychologist who specializes in working with women (and their husbands/partners) on money issues. She is the author of two books, including *It's Only Money: A Primer for Women*, is a contributing editor to Making Bread magazine and is a frequent guest on radio shows.
www.womentalkmoney.com

Carol Adrienne, Ph.D.
The Spiral Path
El Cerrito, CA
Carol is an internationally recognized author and workshop leader whose books appear in over fifteen languages. In private practice, she combines intuitive counseling with life coaching principles to help people recognize and fulfill their life purpose. She has been a numerologist since 1978. Carol's books include, *The Purpose of Your Life; When Life Changes, Or You Wish it Would; Find Your Purpose, Change Your Life* and *The Numerology Kit.* She co-authored with James Redfield, *The Celestine Prophecy: An Experiential Guide* and *The Tenth Insight: An Experiential Guide.*

Her website features a monthly column, blog, numerology charts and a free weekly numerology forecast.
www.CarolAdrienne.com

Elizabeth P. Anderson, CFA
Beekman Wealth Advisory, LLC
New York, NY
Elizabeth P. (Libby) Anderson assists very high net worth private investors and their families in managing all aspects of their financial lives, including asset allocation, asset location, spending, manager selection, and other issues. A wealth advisor to large institutional and private investors since earning her MBA from the Harvard Business School in 1987, Ms. Anderson has written and spoken extensively on these issues, as well as on investing on hedge funds and private equity. She has been in private practice since 2002.

Sharon J. Anderson
Greenbelt, MD
Sharon is an award-winning, independent creative director and writer specializing in storytelling for profit and non-profit organizations. For her work, she has received more than 40 industry awards, including a New York Film Festival Award (non-broadcast) for Short Documentary, featuring 9/11 First Responders, as well as three Gold Addys and two Silver Addys. In addition, in 1985 she was picked out of a Sea World audience to kiss a whale, and in 2001 was awarded Second Place in the Prince George's County Fair Cow Chip Toss. To peruse her video and print work as well as read of her several articles, visit:
www.sharonjanderson.com

Janet Bray Attwood
Enlightened Alliances
Mill Valley, CA
Janet is a speaker, best-selling author and coach for businesses and individuals who want to actualize their passions. Janet is co/founder of Healthy Wealthy n Wise, the #1 online transformational magazine in the world, where she interviews famous transformational leaders once a month on their

passions. She is the author of *The Passion Test.*
www.thepassiontest.com
www.healthywealthynwise.com

Candace Bahr
Bahr Investment Group
Carlsbad, CA
Candace manages money for high-net-worth individuals through Bahr Investment Group/LPL, her own investment management firm. She is co-founder of the non-profit Women's Institute for Financial Education (WIFE.org). Named one of the top ten brokers in the country in 2003 by a national financial trade magazine, Candace is co-author of *It's More Than Money – It's Your Life*.
www.BahrGroup.com

Sue Bates M.Ed.
Seattle, WA
Sue is a licensed therapist with 30 years experience. She specializes in eating disorders and relationship issues. She loves doing groups, as they are so helpful in getting support to move forward with your goals.
www.suebates.com

Sharon Beitzell
Minneapolis, MN
Sharon works with financial advisors in a five-state territory, advising them on market and economic updates and practice management strategies to help them grow their businesses. She also does value-added presentations and seminars for her clients.

Barbara Biziou
Blue Lotus Productions
New York, NY
Barbara is a life coach and leading expert in ritual and practical spirituality. She is the "everyday ritual" expert on New Morning, airing on the Hallmark Channel and is a frequent guest on other radio and national television shows. She consults in person and on the phone. Her books include

The Joy of Ritual and *The Joy of Family Rituals*. She also has a DVD: *Momentary Meditations.*
www.joyofritual.com

Marcia Brixey
Silverdale, WA
Marcia is a popular keynote speaker and President of Money WI$e Women Educational Services, which hosts Money Wi$e Women Forums. She is the author of *Becoming a Money Wi$e Woman: Getting Your Financial House in Order.*
www.marciabrixey.com
www.moneywisewomen.net

Susan Bross, AFC
Susan Bross Financial Counseling
San Rafael, CA.
Susan guides clients toward achieving effortless and effective cash flow serenity and freedom from financial fear.
www.susanbross.com

Deborah Buchta
RMA Consultants
Alamo, CA
Deborah is a real estate marketing consultant as well as a business and personal coach. She is founder of The Brilliance Alliance, a non-profit foundation that fosters positive global change by supporting people who are making a difference in the lives of others, their community and the planet. Her "Introduction to Flocreation" CD was published in 2005.

Chellie Campbell
Author/Speaker
Los Angeles, CA
Chellie, the author of *The Wealthy Spirit* and *Zero to Zillionaire*, is a professional speaker, seminar leader and poker champion. *The Wealthy Spirit* was chosen as a book-of-the-week on the Dr. Laura Schlessinger radio show and a GlobalNet book-of-the-month selection. She has been prominently quoted as a financial expert in Good Housekeeping, Essence, Woman's World, on Lifetime and in more than 15 popular books.

www.chellie.com.

Kellie Carbone, MFT
Oakland, CA
Kellie is a writer and licensed psychotherapist who works with individuals and groups and specializes in helping women to find their unique voice and work through the barriers to manifesting their dreams. She is currently writing a book on this topic, and envisions of a world where more people are inspired to take the risk to live the life of their dreams. She consults in person or by telephone.
www.kelliecarbone.com

Rosemary Davies-Janes
MIBOSO
Canada, U.S. and South Africa
Through her full service Personal Branding Agency, MIBOSO, Rosemary helps intelligent, successful achievers identify and leverage their personal genius to fulfill their potential and their life's purpose. She hosts The Many Faces of Coaching™, a weekly radio show that profiles people who have leveraged their genius to achieve success.
www.miboso.com
www.mibosoradio.com

Sherry J. Davis
Wake Up Coach
Piedmont, CA
Success comes from you! Who you are determines how well what you do works. Understanding who you are is the key to unleashing the power to achieve successful outcomes in your practice and personal life. Together we create your custom-tailored success plan that revolves around YOUR needs and YOUR desires. With 25 years of experience, Sherry is able to partner with you to get results.
www.wakeupcoach.com

Betsy Deak
Create Your Best
Ann Arbor, MI

Betsy works with small business owners, human resource departments, and individuals to get "unstuck" and to maximize efficiency, morale and joy in daily activities. She consults in person, by telephone and email. An award-winning published author, Betsy's work can be accessed on her website. www.CreateYourBest.com.

Pegine Echevarria, MSW
Team Pegine
Ponte Vedra Beach, FL (Jacksonville)
Empowerment guru Pegine Echevarria is described as "bold, brilliant, comical, dynamic, knowledgeable and witty!" Pegine is a leading expert on individual and organizational performance improvement. She is the author of three books including *Sometimes You Have to Kick Your Own Butt*. Pegine appears on CNN, ABC, CBS, NBC, PAX and national radio shows. She is a professional speaker, coach and trainer. Archives of her newsletter are available at: www.pegine.com

Inga Estes, with Cheri Michel
The Coaching Corporation
Santa Monica, CA
The Coaching Corporation is a dynamic business and executive coaching firm created by business owners and executives to facilitate executive and entrepreneurial learning and success. Our clients include Fortune 500 firms, privately held companies and a myriad of small business owners, entrepreneurs, attorneys, CEOs and non-profit organizations. www.TheCoachingCorp.com

Ava Evans, CHt.
Certified Hypnotherapist
Encino, Tarzana and Los Angeles, CA
Using hypnosis, Imagery, Neuro-Linguistic Programming (NLP), Emotional Freedom Technique and other therapies and techniques, Ava helps people gain control of their lives in areas such as depression, smoking cessation, weight control, anxieties, relationship issues and more. Ava also does phone sessions any where in the U.S.

www.Avaevans.com

Tamra Fleming
Architect Your Life, LLC
Seattle, WA
We begin with true life visions and align the interiors of homes and business spaces to match these visions. We call this Intentional Interiors. In addition, we help people live authentic lives by aligning their entire lifestyle to their personal vision. We call this Whole Life Architecture™.
www.architectyourlife.com

Lois P. Frankel, Ph.D.
President, Corporate Coaching International
Pasadena, CA
Dr. Frankel is the author of the international bestsellers *Nice Girls Don't Get the Corner Office* and *Nice Girls Don't Get Rich*. She is also the author of *Overcoming Your Strengths: 8 Reasons Why Successful People Derail and How to Remain on Track* and *Women, Anger & Depression: Strategies for Self Empowerment.* Lois is also a keynote speaker and a featured coach on AOL.com. She can be heard daily in Southern California on KNX 1070 with her coaching tip of the day. Visit her website for more information and free self-inventories.
www.drloisfrankel.com
www.corporatecoachingintl.com

Leah Grant
Inspiration Group, Inc.
U.S.A.
Leah is an international business and marketing strategist and an avid scrapbooker who assists new small business owners in three key areas: 1) who they need to be to be successful, 2) what they need to do to run their business profitably, and 3) how they can market themselves and their products effectively. Get her free Quick Start Business Package and monthly newsletter at her website. She is the co-author of *101 Great Ways to Change Your Life, Volume 2.*
www.leahgrant.com

Nancy Grant
Nancy Grant Coaching, LLC
Portland, OR
Nancy is a Professional Certified Coach and former corporate manager who delights in partnering with women to support their lives and their small businesses. She is particularly passionate about helping women implement the powerful strategies of high income earners through teleclasses, workshops, group coaching, and individual coaching. Nancy works primarily via telephone so is accessible to women world-wide.
www.nancygrantcoaching.com

Rev. Christine Green
Spiritual Director
Portland, OR
Rev. Christine is a spiritual director serving her clients through classes, workshops and personal counseling. Her ministry was founded out of a vision for helping others, especially women, incorporate Universal Truth into their professional and personal lives. Christine is a contributing author to a new anthology, *Pearls of Wisdom: For Living a Richer Life*. She writes a monthly column for the NW Women's Journal called Higher Ground which is archived on her website:
www.sacredheartministries.org

Oriana Green
Writer and web entrepreneur
Diamond Point, WA
In addition to my own creative projects, I assist professionals with their book projects as a ghostwriter, editor and graphic designer. As often as possible, I do my work at the beach.
www.iwriteyourbook.com

Ginger Hilley, M.Ed.
Illumina International
Dallas, TX
Ginger is a "hope" expert who helps people undergo dramatic change in their lives. She addresses clients ranging from physicians, mental health workers, women's groups and

corporations as well as the general public, on topics including: Mindfulness, Self-Care, Psychology of Money, Mental Wealth and numerous wellness themes. She has published articles in medical and grief recovery magazines. Her first book: *Now What?! What to Do When Life Gets in the Way?* is scheduled for publication in 2007.
www.illuminainternational.com

Jan Blakeley Holman CFP, ChFC
Financial Advisor, Smegal & Associates Wealth Management Group of Wachovia Securities
Minneapolis, MN
Jan has 30 years of experience in the financial services industry. The creator of the Financially Empowered Women investment series, she speaks often to audiences on the subjects of successful investing, retirement and leaving a lasting legacy. She and her partners at Smegal & Associates specialize in guiding individuals through the financial, investment and wealth management opportunities created by life's transitions.

Rhonda Hull, Ph.D.
Port Townsend, WA
As a professional speaker, happiness mentor and author of *Drive Yourself Happy*, let Dr. Rhonda Hull act as your "life driving instructor" assisting you to maneuver the road to personal balance, professional success and authentic happiness. She is especially passionate about inspiring women to reclaim their magnificence. Rhonda has what it takes to guide you on your journey, making even the potholes along the way a valuable part of the adventure. She is also the author of the *Manual for Maneuvering Through Life.*
www.driveyourselfhappy.com
www.detourfromstress.com
www.centerofhappiness.com
www.circleconnections.com

Meredyth Hunt
Map of the Hand
Los Angeles, CA

The map of who you are is in your hands. Meredyth decodes crucial information found in the palm and fingerprints relating to your innate strengths and challenges, and she gives practical tools to manage those challenges and navigate you toward your life purpose.
www.mapofthehand.com

Vickie Jenkins
Performance Power Media Coaching
Vickie's clients give highly successful speeches, presentations and media interviews before live audiences and through major media outlets, including: radio, television, magazines and newspapers. Her philosophy: Each of you has a unique and wonderful gift. My job is to inspire you to find it and release it, through communication. The world is waiting for you. Let's fly!
www.media-trainer.com

Elizabeth M. Johnson
E. Johnson & Company
Lakeville, CT
Elizabeth is a Confidence Coach who works exclusively with women on building self-esteem. Described as part teacher, part coach and part best friend, Elizabeth helps women put themselves first, get rid of the shoulds and live their Authentic Self. Her monthly ezine, *In The Pink*, and more can be found on her website:
www.ejohnsonandcompany.com

Laura Handke Jones
Wishweavers
Portland, OR
Laura is the author of *Six Degrees To Your Dreams*. Sign up for her free weekly tips and quarterly newsletter at:
www.wishweavers.com

Sharon Jones
Durham, NC
Sharon provides career advising to college undergraduate and graduate students at a major public university, where she has worked for 15 years. She has also worked with "trailing

spouses" of employees transferred by Fortune 500 companies. Coauthor of *The Parent's Crash Course in Career Planning: Helping Your College Student Succeed*, Sharon has also been an Answer Zone expert on career and graduate school topics for *U.S. News & World Report Online*, and spoken on career topics at national conferences. Sharon earned an M.S. in Industrial Relations from the Krannert Graduate School of Management at Purdue University.
http://home.nc.rr.com/slj/

Jody J. Jungerberg MBA, CFS, ChFC
Savant Capital Management, Inc®.
Rockford, IL
I provide wealth management and financial planning services to high net worth individuals, non-for-profits, institutions and private family offices. I have spent 20+ years in the financial services industry in private banking, trust and portfolio management.

Nikki Kilgore
AccentDigital.com
Los Angeles, CA
Nikki helps clients build successful websites, launch new products/services, and communicate their message effectively. Nikki's award-winning inspirational products have been featured in Glamour, Woman's Day, Complete Woman, Publisher's Weekly, PC Magazine, and have been used by companies such as New Line Cinema, Wells Fargo Bank, America Online and IDG Books (publishers of the "Dummies®" series). Nikki has helped clients such as best-selling author Dr. David Viscott, Comic Relief, and a U.S. presidential campaign candidate.
www.accentdigital.com

Stacey Lane
Career Coach & Consultant
Portland, OR
Stacey loves the challenge of working with bright and talented professionals who are struggling with their career direction and reaching their potential. Whether it's to make more money, find work they love, or to be more successful,

Stacey specializes in helping her clients develop smart and savvy career strategies using an innovative four-step process.
www.staceylane.net

Selma Lewis, Ph.D.
Selma has created a line of Hypnotic CDs to allow everyone to tap the power of their mind.

Lynda Malerstein, C.Ht.
Power Journeys Hypnosis
Los Angeles, CA
Lynda helps adults and children overcome barriers to their success by guiding them to use the power of their deep inner-minds. As they believe it, they achieve it. She is a contributing writer to the book *Everyday Miracles of Hypnotherapy*, the producer of the *Power Journeys Self-Hypnosis* CD series, and has been a frequent featured guest on radio and television. Feel the Freedom of Letting Go!
www.powerjourneys.com

Morgan McCartor
McCartor and Associates
Seattle, WA
Morgan assists organizations in increasing value, flexibility and innovation in services, products, processes and organizational structure. She works with both commercial and non-profit organizations. She has taught systems thinking at Antioch University Seattle and the University of Idaho, Idaho Falls.
www.achievinggreatoutcomes.net

Olivia Mellan
Olivia Mellan &Associates, Inc.
Washington, D.C.
Olivia Mellan is a speaker, author, money coach, psychotherapist and business consultant, and since 1983, she has been a groundbreaker in the field of money psychology and money conflict resolution. Author of four critically acclaimed books, she writes a monthly column, The Psychology of Advice, in Investment Advisor magazine. She's appeared on Oprah, the Today Show and ABC's 20/20

numerous times. She trains counselors, coaches and financial professionals in money psychology tools and recently produced a CD set, The Secret Language of Money.
Her books include: *Money Harmony: Resolving Money Conflicts In Your Life and Relationships*; *Overcoming Overspending: A Winning Plan for Spenders and Their Partners*; *Money Shy to Money Sure: A Woman's Road Map to Financial Well-Being*; and *The Advisor's Guide to Money Psychology.*
www.moneyharmony.com

Sandi Rose Miller
Feng Shui YOUR Way!
Huntington Beach, CA
Sandi is a popular Feng Shui consultant and speaker specializing in simplifying and de-mystifying Feng Shui, making it user-friendly for all. She is the author of *The Art of Living - Feng Shui YOUR Way.*
www.sandirosemiller.com.

Sharon Olson
Olson Weiss, LLC
Minneapolis, MN
Sharon is a Certified Financial Planner with emphasis on estate planning for high net worth families and a personal passion for helping women in retirement and investment planning. Sharon was named in the nation's "Top 100 Exclusive Financial Advisors" by Robb Report Worth Magazine and is a board member of the Ann Bancroft Foundation and The Minnesota State University, Mankato Foundation.
www.olsonweiss.com

Penney Peirce
Penney Peirce Communications
Novato, CA
Penney is an internationally recognized expert intuitive offering intuitive counsel, mentoring, training, lectures and writing. She is the author of *The Intuitive Way, The Present Moment,* and *Dreams for Dummies*.
www.intuitnow.com

Nancy Rosanoff
Pleasantville, NY
Nancy assists individuals and groups understand intuitive intelligence and it's role in making good decisions and in managing projects that work.
She is the author of: *Intuition Workout*, *Knowing When It's Right*, *Making Money Through Intuition*, and *Intuition in the WorkPlace.*
www.rosanoff.com

Harriett Simon Salinger MCC, LCSW
WiseWoman Coaching
Los Angeles CA
The focus of my business is executive and personal coaching. Some people say I'm a practicing wisewoman. My mission in life is to teach people to free themselves from their acquired limitations and take the actions that will free their heart and spirit.
www.hssalinger.com

Jacke L. Schroeder, MSW, LCSW
Ma'at Associates
Portland, OR and Baltimore, MD
Using shamanic practices Jacke consults with corporations, small businesses and non-profits to make better and more informed decisions in all aspects of business, from assessment and planning to decision-making and evaluation. She consults by telephone and in person throughout the country.
www.JackeSchroeder.com

Rhoberta Shaler, Ph.D.
Escondido, CA
Founder, Your Spiritual Home; CEO, Optimize! Institute. Keynotes, seminars, executive coaching. Take an "inspiration break" with this two-minute presentation:
www.TheAffirmativeUniverse.com
www.YourSpiritualHome.com
www.OptimizeInstitute.com

Marci Shimoff
The Esteem Group
San Rafael, CA
Marci Shimoff is a #1 NY Times best selling author of *Chicken Soup for the Woman's Soup 1 & 2, Chicken Soup for the Mother's Soul 1 & 2, and Chicken Soup for the Single's Soul.* Her upcoming release is a breakthrough book on happiness. Marci is an internationally acclaimed keynote speaker specializing in inspiring and transformative programs for women.
www.marcishimoff.com

Bev Sincavage, Ph.D.
Wellness Zen
Middleburg, VA
Bev is a wellness coach and the creator of Healing Alignment TM, a method to relieve the pain of emotional trauma and teach the body to relearn its healing ability through guided imagery and Feng Shui. She is also an artist.
www.wellness-zen.com

Dee Soder, Ph.D.
The CEO Perspective Group
New York, NY
With decades of experience in business and psychology, Dee advises top executives, companies and boards. The pioneer of executive coaching, she is consistently cited by The Wall Street Journal, Fortune Magazine, CNN, CBS Marketwatch, and NBC as "the CEO's coach."
www.ceoperspective.com
www.fastforwardu.com

Nancy D. Solomon, MA
Nancy D. Solomon LLC
Seattle, WA
Nancy is a nationally recognized relationship expert best known for her innovative and provocative work in the human potential field—work that integrates the application of psychology into the practicality of the business environment. Ms. Solomon, a speaker and author, provides

one-on-one and group training, coaching and consulting for executives and their organizations seeking to improve their personal and professional standards of success. She created "It's All About the SHOES: An Invitation for Women to Step into Leadership" a CD Set and "The Courage of Leadership™" window cards. Archives from Nancy's radio spots are available on her website along with the articles she has published.
www.nancydsolomon.com

Barbara Stanny
Barbara Stanny & Co.
Port Townsend, WA
The leading authority on women and money, Barbara has made it her mission to empower women financially. A popular keynote speaker, she appears frequently on national radio and TV shows. She is the author of three bestselling books: *Prince Charming Isn't Coming, How Women Get Smart About Money*; *Secrets of Six-Figure Women, Surprising Strategies to Up Your Earnings and Change Your Life*; *Overcoming Underearning, A Five-Step Plan to a Richer Life.* Barbara is also the co-editor of this anthology. Find all kinds of useful tools at:
www.barbarastanny.com

Terri Jiganti Stewart, CFP
Raymond James & Associates, Inc.
Gig Harbor, WA
Terri works with clients to outline planning needs, establish objectives, determine risk tolerance and develop a financial plan. She is a Certified Financial Planner who provides investment advisory services to individuals, families and small businesses.
www.RaymondJames.com\BushPolen
www.RaymondJames.com/rjfs

Shell Tain, pcc, cpcc
$ensible Coaching
Portland, OR
Shell takes independent business women from the crunch to the ka'ching. Her focus is changing your beliefs and habits

around money as she works with you in an individual or couples format. She's available for speaking presentations and workshops throughout the Pacific Northwest.
www.sensiblecoaching.com

Nita Vallens, Psy.D., LMFT
Psychotherapist and radio show host.
Studio City, CA
Nita provides psychotherapy and hypnotherapy services in person or by phone. She has a weekly radio show, Inner Vision, on KPFK Los Angeles, 90.7 FM which is discussed on her website:
www.nitavallens.com

Mikelann Valterra, MA
The Women's Earning Institute
Seattle, WA
Mikelann is the founder of the Women's Earning Institute and is a specialist in women's earning issues. An author and speaker, her mission is to empower self-employed women to earn what they're really worth, by healing their relationship to money and creating more profitable private practices. Mikelann also runs business support groups and sees private clients. She is the author of *Why Women Earn Less: How To Make What You're Really Worth.*
www.womenearning.com

Ginita Wall
Ginita Wall, CPA, CFP®
San Diego, CA
Ginita is a fee-only financial adviser who guides people through divorce and other financial transitions, such as widowhood and retirement. Ginita has been named to Worth Magazine's list of top financial advisers for seven consecutive years. She is co-founder of the non-profit Women's Institute for Financial Education (WIFE.org), and co-author of *It's More Than Money – It's Your Life.*
www.planforwealth.com

Dina Weinberg
MindLight Group®, LLC

Los Angeles, CA
Dina Weinberg is a consultant and trainer who develops high-performance leaders and highly functioning organizations, focusing on leadership and communications.
Articles featuring Dina have appeared in the Los Angeles Times and in Family Circle.
www.mindlightgroup.com

Vanessa Wesley
BodyVoice Technologies, LLC
Bloomfield Hills, MI
Vanessa is a Certified Practitioner and Trainer of a unique process called the SoulTalk®Method. She is a Reiki Master, and Facilitator of The Work™ by Byron Katie. She helps others make profound and lasting changes quickly and guides them to live in alignment with their purpose. Vanessa works with children and adults, in person or by telephone.
www.bodyvoicetechnologies.com

Marcia Wieder
America's Dream Coach
San Francisco, CA
As America's Dream Coach®, Marcia Wieder travels the world as an ambassador for making dreams real. She's known for giving inspiring talks to notable companies such as American Express, The Gap and Mary Kay. She is actually leading a Dream Movement and is the founder of Dream University® She is the author of *Making Your Dreams Come True, Life is But A Dream,* and *Doing Less and Having More.* She's a columnist for the San Francisco Chronicle, has appeared on Oprah, the Today Show and has been featured in her own PBS-TV show.
www.dreamcoach.com

Breaking Through
is available in these formats:

❂ trade paperback book
❂ e-book
❂ CD: **Ideas To Contemplate from Breaking Through**
❂ MP3 files for **Ideas To Contemplate** with five bonus tracks
❂ CD: **Exercises & Action Steps from Breaking Through**
❂ MP3 files for **Exercises & Action Steps** with five bonus tracks

For more information, visit
www.BreakingThroughBook.com